SPIRIT OF SIOUX FALLS

BY TERRY WOSTER

SPIRIT

SIOUX

BY
TERRY
WOSTER

CORPORATE
PROFILES BY
STEPHEN AND
CATHERINE THURMAN

TOWERY PU

T

O

F

FALLS

ART
DIRECTOR
BRIAN GROPPE

PHOTOGRAPHY
EDITORS
JOEL AND
LAVONNE STRASSER

ISHING, INC.

Acknowledgments

Credit for the narrative of the *Spirit of Sioux Falls* must be spread among many people—some close friends, some formal interview subjects, and many unknown authors of books and articles about the city and its people.

I'd be remiss if I didn't credit, by name, several books I've read and re-read over the years. Included are:

♦ *Sioux Falls, South Dakota, A Pictorial History* by Gary D. Olson and Erik L. Olson.
♦ *Sioux Falls in Retrospect* by R.E. Bragstad.
♦ *Minnehaha County History* by Charles A. Smith.
♦ *Where the Sioux River Bends* by Wayne Fanebust.

In addition, I can't begin to estimate how much of the information and flavor of the city's past I've obtained from the numerous times I've read Bob Karolevitz's history, *Challenge, the South Dakota Story*, and John Milton's flowing bicentennial history, *South Dakota*.

Beyond that, the contributions of present and past staff writers at the *Argus Leader* are immeasurable. Working against constant deadlines, those writers over the years have published an immediate, always changing history of the city.

I'm grateful, too, to *Argus Leader* Publisher Larry Fuller, who allowed me to be part of the *Spirit of Sioux Falls*.

In the past year, I've neglected my wife, Nancy, and children to work some evenings, weekends, or holidays. They've been patient and understanding.

Finally, I offer heartfelt thanks to hundreds of people who've been subjects of interviews during my 25 years in South Dakota journalism. In one way or another, all of them played a part in this project.

Library of Congress Cataloging-in-Publication Data

Woster, Terry.
    The spirit of Sioux Falls / Terry Woster : corporate files by
Stephen and Catherine Thurman.
        p.   cm. — (Urban tapestry series)
    Includes index.
    ISBN 0-9628128-9-7 : $39.50
    1. Sioux Falls (S.D.)—History. 2. Sioux Falls (S.D.)—Pictorial
works. I. Thurman, Stephen, 1950- . II. Thurman, Catherine,
1956- . III. Title. IV. Series.
F659.S6W66 1992
978.3'371—dc20
                                    92-53585
                                       CIP

Towery Publishing, Inc.
1835 Union Avenue, Suite 142
Memphis, Tennessee 38104

Publisher: J. Robert Towery
Editor: Patricia M. Towery
Managing Editor: Michael C. James
Assistant Editor: Allison Jones Simonton
Profile Art Director: Terri J. Jones
Editorial Consultant: John Egan

URBAN TAPESTRY SERIES

TOWERY PUBLISHING, INC.

SIOUX FALLS IS THE ONLY CITY IN SOUTH DAKOTA that belongs to all of us. I truly believe that. Go to the Main Street of any small town in any corner of the state and ask the first 20 people for a Sioux Falls memory. Chances are, they will all have a story ready, almost as if they were just wishing somebody would come along to ask. ◆ Chances are, too, after you've listened to those people, you'll have accumulated 20 very different stories about Sioux Falls. That's because Sioux Falls offers more than any other city or town in South Dakota—and not just commerce, either, although it has more of that than any other population center.

What Sioux Falls has in abundance is variety—in shopping, sports, music, drama, entertainment, education. That's really why it's part of the experience of all South Dakotans. Whatever you seek, you can find it here. I should know. I've been finding memories in the city by the falls of the Big Sioux River for most of five decades.

I've come here as a tourist and a schoolboy, an athlete and a shopper. I've lived here as a working man, and I've been through as a professional journalist on assignment.

I started a family here, and I started a career here. Many of my most important memories have a Sioux Falls setting.

In 1987 when I rejoined the staff of the Sioux Falls *Argus Leader*—the state's largest newspaper in the state's largest city —it felt a lot like I was closing a circle. Even though I continue to live in Pierre managing the *Argus Leader*'s state capitol bureau, returning to the staff of the Sioux Falls newspaper made me feel as if I were coming home to a place I'd never really left.

In the pages that follow, I'm going to tell you a story of Sioux Falls.

I'll do it through the history and geography I've researched, and the people I've known, interviewed, and shared this city with during more than a quarter century of newspaper work in South Dakota.

Framed by the window of a nearby building, the Old County Courthouse stands as one of Sioux Falls' instantly recognized landmarks, home now to the Siouxland Heritage Museum.

To understand the city, you must know where it came from. That's the history.

You must appreciate the environment that gives Sioux Falls its unique sense of place. That's the geography.

You must recognize the background of the folks who settled here, and the

> "There's a civic spirit, a kind of aggressive leadership that, once it develops in a town, is passed on through generations," says Thomas Kilian, a longtime resident. That's the Sioux Falls spirit.

ones who came later to build on what those homesteaders had begun. That's the people.

Most of all, to understand this city, you must recognize that there's something called the Sioux Falls spirit.

Some time back, I interviewed Thomas Kilian, a longtime Sioux Falls resident who's spent a considerable part of his life pondering where the city came from, where it's headed, and how it came to prominence among South Dakota communities.

Kilian is convinced that any city worthy of the name develops a personality of its own and tends to attract people of that personality type. Sioux Falls has a spirited personality, Kilian says. From its first days as a bend-in-the-river tent town to its head-first dive into the 21st century, it has always attracted society's developers, boosters, and risk takers, people whose drive and success in turn made the city successful.

"There's a civic spirit, a kind of aggressive leadership that, once it develops in a town, is passed on through generations," he says.

That's the Sioux Falls spirit.

In the pages that follow, I think that quality will be more than evident. I can't always define it in precise phrases, but I know it when I see it. As we go further, I think I can help you see and feel it, too.

It's a cinch the people at *Money* magazine recognized it.

The September 1992 issue of the magazine declared Sioux Falls the best place in the nation to live. Few who are familiar with the city would disagree. *Money* cited Sioux Falls' 2.6 percent unemployment rate and said it had "one of the most diverse and robust economies anywhere in the U.S." The magazine also gave the city top marks for health care, housing, and ease of travel.

Of course, *Money* wasn't the first magazine to become aware of the Sioux Falls phenomenon. The city has been big news in the '90s. For example:

—A national truck rental company ranked Sioux Falls sixth in the country for the ratio of people moving into town to those leaving.

—A regional publication of the Federal Reserve Bank of Minneapolis called Sioux Falls one of its 15 super cities, a modest-sized community with the good things in life close at hand.

—*Kiplinger's Personal Finance Magazine* called the city one of the 15 best for job hunters and for people starting or relocating a business.

As we look closer at the city, I think I'll be able to show you some features that might have caught the attention of *Money* and those other publications, some of the things that make it possible for Sioux Falls to live up to its new slogan: "America's Best Place to Live."

First, I'd like to set the stage by telling you the story of Sioux Falls that I promised a bit earlier. It's a story of a man and his love for a city he's known all his life.

If it seems highly personal, it is. It's my story. I have a hunch, though, that it could be yours, too. It could be the story of anyone who's lived here or worked here, gone to college or vocational school here, bought a car or a prom dress here. Any of those people could tell the story, in their own way and their own words.

Like the city itself, the story of Sioux Falls belongs to all of us.

MY FIRST VISIT TO SIOUX FALLS WAS A RELIGIOUS experience. Really. ♦ I can't recall exactly how old I was, but my family still lived on a Lyman County farm west of the Missouri River, which fairly bisects the state. We'd just gotten a new Nash—the classic model shaped like an overturned bathtub—and a journey of nearly 150 miles on old U.S. Highway 16 from Reliance to Sioux

Falls was something that took most of a week to consider and at least a day to prepare for.

We traveled 18 miles to Chamberlain frequently and 88 miles to Mitchell now and then. But nothing in my experience with either of those cities prepared me for Sioux Falls. Even then, at least 40 years ago, it seemed a metropolis.

We came to Sioux Falls to witness a religious ceremony at St. Joseph's Cathedral. A number of new priests were taking their final vows in the Roman Catholic faith, I believe.

Of the ceremony I recall little. A number of young men in white robes lay full-length on their faces on the stone floor of the church. Thick marble columns soared toward a high, arched ceiling that seemed to disappear beyond the hanging lights.

What I do remember is how the city looked from the front steps of the cathedral. Situated high on a hill in one of the old sections of town, the cathedral was as fine a vantage point as there was to appreciate Sioux Falls. It still is.

Even at that early age, I loved what I saw. The immediate neighborhood was rich with huge, old homes. The clock tower rose above the rooftops at the northern border of downtown, and

Framed by the porch pillars of a nearby home, the spires of St. Joseph's Cathedral soar 185 feet in the air. The Roman Catholic cathedral has been a Sioux Falls landmark since 1918 (opposite). The rich backdrop of a sunset fading from orange to violet (preceding pages) silhouettes the downtown skyline of Sioux Falls, showcased in 1992 by *Money* magazine as the best place in the nation to live.
Antonio Sanchez photo

homes and businesses stretched far into the distance beyond the lush trees that bordered the river.

How could a kid from the prairie not love this city?

When I was growing up halfway across the state, Sioux Falls was the fastest-growing city in South Dakota. On a variety of trips there with my family, I learned to enjoy the busy downtown— Fantle's and Shriver's and

> The clock tower rose above the
> rooftops at the northern border
> of downtown, and homes and
> businesses stretched far into the
> distance beyond the lush trees that
> bordered the river.
> How could a kid from the prairie
> not love thi s city?

Woolworth's, Weatherwax (where some years later under the watchful eye of a fiscally conservative father, I bought my first sportcoat), and Montgomery Ward and Co. (where years after the sportcoat business, my wife and I bought our first crib.)

Of enormous interest to a school kid my age was Washington High School, the biggest school in the state. To those of us who grew up in small towns, Washington High always seemed to have the biggest football players, the smartest students, and the fastest quarter milers.

The athletes who wore Washington's orange and black made quite an impression. Fred Hecker paced a string of unbeaten Warrior football teams in the 1950s. Bob Johnson sprinted with the speed and grace of a prairie deer. Freckle-faced, red-haired Dick Callahan was a state track champion in the middle distances and a gridiron ace

who continued his football at the University of Nebraska.

But athletics was just a part of the Washington High mystique. The place produced political leaders, including Republican Gov. George Mickelson, elected in 1986 and voted in for a second term in 1990.

Mickelson is only one of three governors with Washington High diplomas. The late Nils Boe, who served from 1965 to 1969, went from the statehouse to the White House as intergovernmental relations specialist under President Richard Nixon. Boe then accepted an appointment as chief justice of the U.S. Customs Court in New York.

Joe Foss, governor from 1955 to 1959, is a true South Dakota legend. A Marine fighter pilot, he was World War II's first flying ace. Foss tied World War I hero Eddie Rickenbacker's record by shooting down 26 Japanese airplanes while serving at Guadalcanal in 1942 and 1943.

Gov. Mickelson, who moved to Sioux Falls from Selby before entering high school, once said that one of the best parts about being a teenager in Sioux Falls was the city's dual personality. It had the comfortable, neighborly feeling of any small town in South Dakota, he said, but it also had a big-city attitude toward providing all the goods and services, culture, and entertainment that city life demanded.

For instance, the ballrooms and dance halls people talked about throughout the region were in Sioux Falls. They booked the best big bands, the hottest country acts, and the freshest rock groups.

When rock and roll swept the country and out-of-the-way places like Lubbock, Texas, and Fargo, North Dakota, were producing the likes of Buddy Holly and Bobby Vee, Sioux Falls produced its own contribution to the new music wave. Myron Lee, a Washington High School product, formed a band called the Caddies that fronted for many of the top names in rock across the nation. Now, maybe Myron Lee and the Caddies never made the big time, but they still knock 'em dead on frequent road trips and at their popular New Year's Eve show in downtown Sioux Falls.

Since the '60s, when I saw my first country concert at the Sioux Falls Arena—Johnny Cash and the Tennessee Three, George Jones, Grandpa Jones, and a quartet of newcomers, the Statler Brothers—Sioux Falls' own Bob Alley has earned a reputation writing and playing a personal brand of country. Bands like American Made and I-90 West filled the void when Alley took his talents to Nashville.

In recent years, local nightclubs have booked more national blues and jazz acts to meet the growing demand. Local groups like Chord On Blue bring a South Dakota flavor to the blues, while Flag With Hank and Janitor Bob and the Armchair Cowboys have emerged as hot rock and roll bands that tour the region from a Sioux Falls base.

This all goes to show that Sioux Falls has always been where the traveling shows stop and the good bands originate. Of course, Sioux Falls was where all the latest trends—the fads and fashions— reached South Dakota.

The first hula hoop I ever saw was being twirled by a dark-haired school girl on a downtown street corner near the old Lemond's restaurant. Some years later and little more than a block from that site, I first sighted a miniskirt. Bell-bottoms, Beatle boots, and Nehru jackets were sported here, too.

Sioux Falls always had the most popular drive-in restaurants, places like the Barrell with car hops and root beer, and the state's early pizza joints, like Charlie's, where the college crowd used to hang out.

High school kids packed their parents' Chevys and Fords to cruise town, "doing the loop," as they called it, for hours on end—each rider pitching in a few coins so the driver could pump a buck's worth of gas. The price of gas has gone up, but the kids still do the loop every evening.

Sioux Falls was also the sports Mecca of the state, where every March unknown kids from small schools like Alexandria and Hayti and Fort Pierre would find out what it was like to play basketball with nearly 10,000 people watching each of three days at the state Class B tournament.

Few thrills in high school sports can match that of playing in the old "B" tournament in the Sioux Falls Arena, but running on the track at Howard Wood Field comes close. The annual Dakota Relays each spring attracts the best high school and college athletes in the region. The times are fast, the jumps high, the throws long.

In the late '50s and early '60s, Sioux Falls hosted the NAIA track and field national finals, bringing world-class college performers together in a show of talent unmatched in the upper Mid-

Sioux Falls' economy has expanded and diversified, but agriculture remains a strong base. Here, modern-day farmers show how the wheat harvest used to take place in the days of the steam threshing machines.

west. Two athletes in particular come to mind.

Bob Hayes, later a wide receiver with the Dallas Cowboys, staked his claim to the title of World's Fastest Human on the Wood track in 1961, running a world record-tying 9.3 seconds in the 100-yard dash. Fans who packed the stadium that evening will remember the long delay while disbelieving officials measured and re-measured the track to verify the distance.

Ralph Boston, 1960 Olympic long jump champion, won four individual events and placed second in another during the 1961 NAIA final. The image I remember, though, is of Boston signing autograph after autograph, then—with a huge grin on his face— loping across the Howard Wood infield with a pack of youngsters at his heels, each wanting him to sign just one more program.

Of thousands of such simple moments is the love for a city written in a young man's heart.

But that's worship from afar. To really learn to love the city, I had to live here. I got that chance in 1967.

Anson Yeager, a transplanted ranch kid from Meade County who'd become executive editor of the *Argus Leader*, took a chance and hired me as a photographer. Flush with that success, my new bride and I could only marvel at the unlimited opportunities in this new, exciting city of ours when she also found a full-time job, working as a registered nurse at McKennan Hospital.

We found a tiny home on the quiet edge of McKennan Park, so close to the hospital's front door we were able to walk there one early December morning a few hours before our daughter was born. In those early days of our marriage, it seemed we always had time to bundle our baby girl into a stroller and walk through the old neighborhood, admiring the majestic homes and trees, kicking through piles of leaves at the curbs.

Those were the carefree times. At work, I was busy learning about the city. Few occupations offer a young person more chances for an education in the geography, history, current events, and social study of a city than does that of newspaper photographer.

In my years at the *Argus Leader* the first time around, I was all over Sioux Falls. I shot pictures of children in their first dance recital at the old Coliseum and senior citizens at birthday parties honoring a century of living. Bake sales, book fairs, symphonies, and football games were photo assignments that took me from one border of the city to the other, as did summer droughts, snowstorms, and spring floods.

One stormy day I photographed hundreds of volunteers filling sandbags as the Big Sioux boiled closer and closer to the rim of its banks and rumors spread that the dam above the city was all but played out.

Another morning I stood with a group of civic dreamers atop a downtown bank building. They were local business leaders using the vantage point of the building's roof to study the existing layout of the city. A banker named Tom Reardon pointed off into the distance and said, "Someday, the town will stretch twice as far." I took a number of photographs that morning and I listened well, but my camera couldn't begin to capture their visions of Sioux Falls' future—visions which are now being fulfilled.

Still another assignment took me nearly 70 miles west, to the James River near Mitchell. There I photographed Governor Boe and a collection of Sioux Falls and Mitchell dignitaries in a ceremony dedicating the Interstate 90 bridge. Completion of that bridge late in 1967 meant freeway travel ▶ was possible from Chamberlain all the way to Sioux Falls, a distance of some 120 miles.

At the time, the dedication ceremony seemed just another photo assignment for a 24-year-old and a chance to see the governor up close. Reflecting on it now, I understand what those leaders saw back then: Every mile of interstate completed meant faster and safer travel to Sioux Falls. That meant more visitors, more demands, and more opportunities for medical centers, shops and stores, theaters, sports centers, and stockyards. With the completion of both Interstate 90 west to Wyoming and Interstate 29 from Nebraska to North Dakota, Sioux Falls in the 1970s became easily accessible to anyone within 400 miles.

I didn't realize it at the time, but what I was seeing through my camera's viewfinder on that bridge 25 years ago was a picture of coming growth. The city was poised for progress.

Shortly before I moved from Sioux Falls for a job in Pierre, I drove west over the two-lane blacktop of 41st Street to the edge of town for an interview at O'Gorman High School. I've often wished I'd taken pictures of my route that day. The lens would have captured a field of dark-green corn thriving not so very far from the spot where today the Empire mall anchors South Dakota's most heavily traveled and intensely commercial thoroughfare.

Driving that same but vastly altered 41st Street these days, I approach the O'Gorman corner at the intersection of Kiwanis Avenue and marvel at the incredible spirit that pushed the city in so few years so far beyond the limits of anything I'd have dreamed possible.

The spirit isn't diminishing, either. Far from it.

I have read the projections of the city planners, the newest generation of Sioux Falls dreamers. They predict a city bursting at its seams—a population of 100,814 adding people at a rate of nearly 2,500 people a year through the first decade and a half of the 21st century.

Where once it appeared the city's boundaries might be limited to a top-heavy triangle roughly defined by Marion Road, Highway 38, and

LLOYD CUNNINGHAM

A true crossroads, Kiwanis Avenue and 12th Street. A right turn here will take you past the Great Plains Zoo, and out to 41st Street's commercial strip. Straight ahead is the shortest route to the downtown financial and business district.

Interstate 229, now planners see the newcomers following Horace Greeley's advice to "Go West." But many will look south, too, and east, spreading the metropolitan area of the state's biggest city as far as enthusiasm and optimism can carry them.

The growth will be fueled by people not so different from the first Sioux Falls settlers. The early Scandinavians and Germans and Irish came to the area because they saw opportunity—shops to be opened and land broken to the plow. New growth is being spurred by the spiritual descendants of those pioneers. There are still businesses to open and jobs to be filled. More than that, there are schools and parks, museums and movie theaters, playhouses and concert symphonies, art festivals and athletic events to cement that strong sense of community so important in the upper Midwest.

Some years ago, a newspaper editor approaching middle age told me he envied me a great deal. The news business was on the verge of incredible change, and I was young enough to be part of it, while he would miss much of it.

I look at the Sioux Falls I knew 40 years ago and the city I see today, and I understand what that editor was saying. I'm not so old that I won't be around for at least some of that change, but I know I'll never outlast the spirit that keeps the city moving. For in spite of decades of tremendous progress, Sioux Falls is poised for more incredible change and growth.

The city has taken a strong step toward guaranteeing continued commercial development with Forward Sioux Falls, a marketing effort started in 1988 that raised more than $4 million in four years to promote the city.

But in addition to business growth, I see Sioux Falls poised to begin what University of South Dakota historian and novelist John Milton has called the struggle for culture. Having established a firm economic base, planned its roads, bridges, sewers, and water systems, and drafted a long-range plan for the city's education needs, Sioux Falls is in a position to turn its attention toward further development of the arts and culture, the things that fill the human spirit. A performing arts center surely is just over the horizon.

I also see in Sioux Falls' continuing cultural development a long look back to document and appreciate its rich heritage, both the histories of the settlers and the variety of Indian tribes that have been and continue to be part of the Sioux Falls story.

I envy the people who will have the opportunity to live with and love the city in the next four decades the way I have for the last four.

They have an experience ahead of them the likes of which dreams are made.

THE WATERFALLS OF THE BIG SIOUX RIVER CREATE A fascinating place, the natural heart of the city. History books will tell you that. So will any kid in town. ◆ To youngsters, the falls is one grand park—a play area, a deep-woods adventure for 20th century explorers, a fishing hole, a nature trail and, to the dismay of parents in every corner of the city, a swimming hole. ◆ Go to Falls Park and see

for yourself. You'll stand on damp rocks in the shade of huge old trees, watching and listening as the swiftly moving water gurgles over rough, red rocks and foams in the deep pool at the foot of the falls. The sound is as much a magnet for youngsters as is the calliope on a circus wagon.

Is it any wonder the falls had the same effect on the first inhabitants in this part of the world?

The Big Sioux River Valley was formed centuries ago, as the last great ice age drew to a close. Massive glaciers cut deeply into the quartzite bedrock, creating the falls and depositing the clay loam soil that was to become some of the most productive farm land in South Dakota. Around the newly formed river valley the land stretched unbroken to the horizon. It was gently rolling prairie, largely treeless, with thick, stubborn grass that rippled in the wind like the surface of a gigantic lake. On that broad plain, the only shelter from weather and protection from predators would be found among the tree-lined bluffs of the Big Sioux River.

Historians can't pinpoint the first time the combination of precious shelter and plentiful water drew a human to the falls, but they suggest that for perhaps 1,500 years the banks have been the site of a settlement of one sort or another.

Indians sometimes referred to as Mound Builders were among the first to leave signs of their passing. In the upper Big Sioux River valley and further west along the James River, natives left burial mounds, some of which can still be seen in Sherman Park. The story goes that curious soldiers at old Fort

The story of Sioux Falls begins where the community began, at the picturesque falls of the Big Sioux River.

Dakota, established in 1865, sometimes dug into the mounds. In the 1870s early townsmen Richard and Fred Pettigrew unearthed bits of pottery and stone tools that later became part of an artifacts collection donated to the city.

Sometime after 800 A.D., Indians identified as ancestors of the Mandan established villages in the area of the falls. They were followed by the Lakota Sioux, who'd been pushed west out of their traditional hunting grounds by

The Big Sioux River valley was formed centuries ago, as the last great ice age drew to a close. Massive glaciers cut deeply into the quartzite bedrock, creating the falls and depositing the clay loam soil that was to become some of the most productive farm land in South Dakota.

tribes bearing primitive rifles obtained from white traders.

The falls of the Big Sioux weren't to remain a home for the Indians, however. President Thomas Jefferson saw to that in 1803, when he negotiated the Louisiana Purchase and sent Meriwether Lewis and William Clark to explore the region.

The Lewis and Clark journey was the first of numerous private and government-sponsored expeditions into the territory. History books offer contradictory stories of the first non-Indians to reach the falls. Some argue it was French scientist Joseph Nicolas Nicollet during an 1838 mapping excursion. Others say it's more likely Army Capt. Joseph Allen's 1844 visit was first.

Whichever story is true, the result was the same. People came. Men and

women of strong spirit and big dreams in the already settled cities back East read the journals kept by the first explorers, and they immediately saw opportunity.

Historian Milton wrote: "Everyone knew, or should have known...that the middle part of the continent was almost a desert, that the weather was foul, that Indians roamed the plains and that uncivilized dangers lay at every—every what? There were no corners, no bends in the road, no roads, no hills, not even a landmark to finish the phrase. They came mostly for the last free land on the continent."

In the 1850s, the promise of land drew fair-haired Swedes and Norwegians, thick-muscled Germans, Dutch, and Irish. They were confident that hard work would turn the prairie into fields thick with wheat and corn. The harvested wheat would turn mill wheels, the ripened corn would feed cattle and pigs. New families would require supply and hardware stores, schools, and churches.

Sioux Falls was founded during this heady time of land speculation and western expansion when nothing seemed impossible to people willing to take a risk. And keen competition was a part of the spirit that was around from the beginning.

In 1856, two rival groups of speculators—the Dakota Land Company of St. Paul, Minnesota, and the Western Land Company of Dubuque, Iowa—rushed to claim a piece of the treasure described in the journals of Nicollet and Capt. Allen. The companies arrived within days of each other, but a few days made a difference. The Dubuque group was first and claimed 320 acres around the falls. The St. Paul company put its claim in above the falls.

Those companies hoped the force of the rushing water would power commerce, but they were wrong. Oh, folks tried to make the falls work for them. Some succeeded, for a time, but not long enough to make milling or hydroelectric generation the real foundation of Sioux Falls.

The Queen Bee Mill—a seven-story monster capable of processing 1,200 barrels of flour a day—opened in 1881 at the falls. Historians suggest the area didn't produce enough wheat to keep the mill operating at a profit, and it closed in 1883. Although the business lasted only two years, the shell of a building that remains on the bank of the river today is a reminder of the first, failed effort to harness the Big Sioux.

Not far from the Queen Bee and just about the time the old mill closed, the Drake Polishing Works opened. It lasted into the early years of the 20th century, polishing quartzite and petrified wood.

Around 1883, a less ambitious mill than the Queen Bee began using the Big Sioux flow to grind wheat into flour. A.E. Sherman, a transplanted Massachusetts teacher whose devotion to the betterment of Sioux Falls eventually earned him the title "Father of the Park System," convinced a group of investors to join him in buying that smaller operation, the Cascade Mill. In 1887 the foresighted group also built an electrical generating plant at the mill. Powered by steam, that generator produced the city's first alternating current just in time to put a gleam in the first incandescent bulbs the area had seen.

In spite of those modest riverside successes, the falls as a source of power never became the economic force the early speculators had hoped it would be. They began to see that the future—economic prosperity and stability—lay in the city's ability to become a transportation and business hub.

The ability of 19th century Sioux Falls business leaders to see the wisdom in economic diversity gave the city a big edge on the dozens of competing communities that seemed to spring up overnight as the nation moved west.

Early on, it had appeared that other cities might win. To backtrack a little, no sooner had Sioux Falls been settled in the 1850s than it had to be abandoned in 1862. The threat of Indian attacks forced residents to accept a military escort to Yankton, and the townsites were left empty, soon to be burned.

It may have been the last time the people of Sioux Falls backed away from a fight.

Three years after the soldiers marched the city's few residents out of town, a settlement was re-established with the Army's help. Townspeople had

convinced the military it was in the public interest to establish a fort at the old site. How else could people feel safe to settle the lush river valley?

In 1865, Fort Dakota was created, covering an area that today would run between 7th and 9th streets along Phillips Avenue, a location that would become the heart of present-day downtown.

The fort only lasted five years, but its existence was vital to the growth of Sioux Falls. Not only did the soldiers' presence help settlers breathe more

A look back at Sioux Falls around 1888 reveals the view west along 6th Street (above) and northwest from 6th Street (opposite).

easily, but the Army built solid barracks and outposts capable of standing long after the military was gone.

No sooner had the soldiers moved out than the settlers moved in. Enterprising locals converted the empty fort buildings into a store, a schoolhouse, and a post office.

Among the settlers who found space in the old military buildings was Dr. Josiah L. Phillips. If you wonder how a person gets a major city street named after him, look no further for answers than the story of J.L. Phillips.

Phillips was a Chicago Medical School graduate and a Civil War surgeon sent to Sioux Falls by the Western Land Company, the Dubuque half of the dueling investment companies. By the time the military began to phase out operations at Fort Dakota, the original land companies had ceased to be a factor in the city's development. But Sioux Falls was rich with potential for those with gumption enough to claim a piece of the action, and several former officers of the two land companies tried.

In the scramble for property, Phillips shrewdly managed to claim for himself about a quarter-section of land. It turned out to be a nifty little package, too, including the fort site and most of what's now downtown Sioux Falls. To add to his fortune, when the Army sold the fort buildings in 1870, Phillips was the only bidder.

In 1870 and 1871, Phillips laid out lots and marked streets in his newly acquired property, putting on paper for the first time the grid system that remains the layout of the city between 6th and 9th streets from Phillips to Minnesota Avenue.

People in a booming city sometimes complain about the mess of construction and the frantic pace of expansion.

But the Sioux Falls of 1870 must have had the grand-daddy of all construction jams. When Phillips mapped out his downtown, the streets and blocks on paper didn't match the buildings and streets of Fort Dakota. New buildings were subsequently located according to Phillips' official system, while old fort buildings had to be torn down.

Richard F. Pettigrew, a student surveyor turned town booster, is credited with putting up one of the first new buildings. Armed with a law degree from a college in Wisconsin, he came to

in on a good thing, sort of the way they are these days. They were. By the end of 1873, nearly 600 people called Sioux Falls home. That was growth of more than 500 in three short years. The development-minded city fathers must have been overwhelmed by the city's frantic pace, and those plucky 600 must have patted themselves on the back, asking, can anything stop the progress?

It sure could. A plague of grasshoppers and an economic depression hit the city together. Money virtually disappeared and took with it the new

nies followed suit. The combination of plentiful rainfall, better financial conditions nationwide, and dependable rail service started Sioux Falls on a 20-year growth spurt.

Historians call that time the "Dakota Boom," and for Sioux Falls it truly was. The city grew at a rate of 1,000 people a year. The 1890 census counted 10,167, and some said only low market prices for farm commodities kept that figure from being even more impressive.

The Dakota Boom changed Sioux Falls from an overgrown prairie town with dirt streets into a sophisticated city. During the years between 1878 and 1900 a water system was begun, first using the river as a source, but later moving to a well field north of town. Electric street lights and gas lamps were added, and Phillips Avenue was paved, using quartzite stone from local mines. Pettigrew started a streetcar company and began planning what eventually was the forerunner of the present Sioux Falls Stockyards. The Minnehaha County Courthouse went up at 6th and Main. Local leaders won a fierce contest of political wills to become the county seat.

Sioux Falls in 1869 and within two years owned a small office building on Phillips just north of 8th Street.

Shortly after Pettigrew's building was finished, Harry Corson arrived in town and put up a fine hotel at 9th and Phillips. The Cataract Hotel became famous for its fancy accommodations, and farm kids in for a day in the city used to marvel at a place with that many rooms, an elevator, and a dining room, all under one roof. After the Cataract went up, it attracted a second hotel nearby, the Central House, and then the elegant Van Eps, which would become a landmark.

With all that economic activity, you'd expect that people would have been just swarming to Sioux Falls to get

businesses, new farms, and promised railroad service that was supposed to be the linchpin in Sioux Falls prosperity.

By historical standards, the downturn was brief, just five years. But for those five years the city's population figures didn't budge, and Sioux Falls remained a one-street town. Before the good times returned in 1878, the spirit of Sioux Falls had been severely tested. The city would face an even sterner test during the Great Depression of the 1930s, and repeated, though perhaps less widespread, downturns in the mid-1980s, but that was over the horizon.

In the 1878 revival, rain was falling on farm fields and the St. Paul and Sioux City Railroad Company soon steamed into town. Other rail compa-

The boom brought increased concern for the overall welfare of Sioux Falls citizens, and in 1881 the city offered a group of Baptists a free building site for a college, the forerunner of Sioux Falls College. In 1889, a Lutheran school opened that became Augustana College.

The first hospital opened in 1901 at 19th and Minnesota and operated until 1930, when the present Sioux Valley Hospital began caring for patients. In addition, McKennan Hospital opened in 1911 when the Presentation Sisters of Aberdeen agreed to manage the facility, boosting the city's growing reputation as a medical center. Both hospitals have grown to be among the city's largest employers and the region's most dependable sources of health care.

In the 1900s, growth occurred in all directions. Downtown filled in with city hall, the federal building, banks, law offices, and retail merchants. Neighborhoods spread out from the heart of town, each springing up around a community focal point—a grade school, a park, a hospital, or a landmark.

Radio and, later, television helped spread the Sioux Falls story across the state and into Minnesota and Iowa. Midcontinent Broadcasting in particular was quick to see the economic advantage of telecasting to the widest possible audience. Transmitting towers in Garden City and Reliance helped spread the message of KELO-TV, the city's first television station. Soon after

the city completed a transportation circle that guaranteed continued and increased commerce.

People traveling by car can go wherever they wish, and Sioux Falls began to venture farther from downtown in the 1960s. Completion of Western Mall in 1968 changed traditional traffic patterns and shopping habits forever.

shops. It isn't the merchandising hub that 41st has become. Instead, it has become a place with its own charm, a mixture of new construction and fine old buildings.

Any talk of downtown would be woefully incomplete without at least touching on the history the area has had of rebounding from huge fires. The community struggled in 1991 to recover

Sioux Falls has developed into a regional center for commerce and health care, as well as for enterprising business leaders such as *Tri-State Neighbor* publisher Bill Byrne (center), whose success story was a cover feature of *Fortune* magazine.

KELO entered the television business, Mort Henkin, owner of KSOO radio, followed suit, and the city's place as the head of the region in electronic journalism was secure.

In the 1960s, passenger service by rail was declining. For many South Dakota towns that meant trouble. Not so in Sioux Falls. The national network of interstate highways—I-29 going north and south, and I-90 east and west—formed a giant intersection at the northwest edge of town, and I-229 looping around the southeast edge of

More businesses opened on 41st Street near the Western Mall. Fewer businesses stayed downtown. The Empire mall, completed in 1975, pulled traffic even farther west along 41st, and other retailers rushed to fill the gaps along the new business thoroughfare.

Property values soared as the traffic swelled. A 1992 count showed as many as 50,000 cars a day traveled 41st Street. A local businessman who once had a chance to buy land along the strip for under $10,000 still shakes his head when he sees that it's grown in value to more than $250,000.

That rush to the strip left downtown Sioux Falls groping for a new identity. The area where the Sioux Falls spirit first took hold has been gradually redefining itself over the past two decades. Today downtown is a mixture of banks and financial services, office buildings, restaurants, and specialty

from a blaze that destroyed the Hanson Building at the corner of 11th and Phillips. The three-story building burned much of a Saturday in May, but by afternoon on Sunday city leaders were talking about rebuilding.

The Hanson Building fire was the most recent in a list of historic downtown blazes, the first of which started 91 years earlier and two blocks away. In 1900, the Cataract Hotel fire was blamed on fireworks. Other major fires destroyed the old *Argus Leader* building at 109 N. Main in 1951, the Dakota Warehouse at 415 N. Weber in 1981, Foremost Dairy at 2nd and Main in 1987, and Shipley's Launderers at 213 W. 9th in 1988.

Sioux Falls recovered from each of those fires, just as it had bounced back for more than a century from grasshoppers, floods, blizzards, and drought.

Presently, Sioux Falls is growing at a rate of about 600 people—a city the size of Sioux Falls in 1873—every three months. The population is projected to reach 150,000 by the year 2015, up more than 48,000 from the 1990 census. If that isn't enough to make Josiah Phillips envious, projections suggest the next two decades will see another 10 square miles, as much as 6,700 acres, devoted to residential development. That could mean a city stretching from

economy is built on a broad base. Examine the top 10 employers in town: John Morrell, a meat packing plant; Citibank, a credit card company; Sioux Valley and McKennan hospitals; Midwest Coast Transport, a trucking company; Hutchinson Technology, a computer parts manufacturer; Hy-Vee Food Stores and Sunshine Food Markets, grocery chains; Good

town Sidewalk Arts Festival, and the Northern Plains Tribal Arts exhibit, which draws Indian artists from across the plains each year to show and sell their works, bring the whole community out in support of the region's fine talents.

Today at the falls, it takes only a little imagination to stand at the edge of the rushing water and get a sense of the

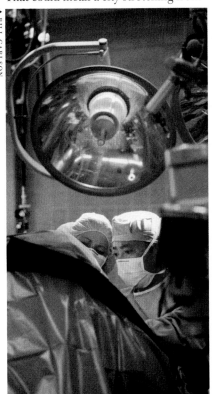

BILL CARLSON

ROD JONES

THE ARGUS LEADER

Whether it's the urgency of the operating room, the excitement of a street fair, or the bustle of construction, such as work on the 11th Street viaduct, Sioux Falls is a vibrant community.

Interstate 90 south to the Tea Road and from the Ellis Road east to state Highway 11. That core area Phillips laid out 120 years ago begins to look mighty small smack in the middle of all this growth.

An aggressive economic development posture—responsible in part for the decision by Citibank to locate its national credit-card operations in the city in 1981—has kept Sioux Falls at the forefront of business and industrial growth through the last decades of the 20th century.

The lessons of early Sioux Falls developers have been heeded: The

Samaritan Society, a provider of care for the elderly; and Raven Industries, a manufacturer of plastic, electronic, and sewn products.

State tax policy has helped Sioux Falls grow, too. The largest city in a state without a personal or corporate income tax is sure to get a second look when a corporation is thinking of expanding or relocating.

Although a strong economic base is a major source of pride, Sioux Falls today is much more than an account of its business activity. The city regularly sells out its Community Concert series. The Sioux Falls Community Playhouse each season offers a lively mix of comedy, drama, and musicals. Local colleges and high schools add variety with bands and vocal groups, as well as their own stage productions.

Such events as the Friends of Traditional Music concerts, the down-

hope and the potential the first settlers must have felt as they stood on the same spot and dreamed of the future.

When I think of that spirit, I consider how fitting it is that the same boldness should continue to be the strong backbone of this community's character more than a century later.

The history of Sioux Falls is being written day after day, and no single piece of good news is enough to make the city sit back satisfied with what it has accomplished. Even so, *Money* magazine's choice of Sioux Falls as the best place in the country to live is one sign that the effort hasn't gone unnoticed.

Best of the nation's top 300 cities. Now there's one for the history books.

WE'VE COVERED AT LEAST 15 CENTURIES IN THE past few pages, from the days when the first unknown Indian tribes knew of the Big Sioux River and its falls to the last days of the 20th century. That's a pretty good jaunt in a short space. ◆ Pretty soon, we're going back to the falls at the end of another kind of journey through Sioux Falls. I'd like to show you a few sights of

the town, take you to some places that are recognized landmarks, and point out a few of the newer parts of town that are likely to become landmarks in the next generation or two.

To get you in the mood for that excursion, I'm going to introduce you to a few more places and people I've come to know around here, the kind of places that say Sioux Falls to me and the kind of people I've somehow linked with the city.

This part of the story starts early in the day, right around sunrise. Most of the city is just beginning to rise and stretch, but the pace is already frantic at the Sioux Falls Stockyards. Cattle snort and moan as they're driven into a holding pen. Sheep bleat while high-booted workers from the yards whistle or clap their hands to keep the animals moving from truck to pen to market.

A visitor not acquainted with the layout of the place might stand on the high catwalks and see a huge confusing maze of activity, but the drivers who piloted the 18-wheelers of Hereford and Angus steers know exactly what's happening. So do the buyers and sellers. They know who's bringing in Hereford steers today and which ranch shipped the pen of ebony-colored Angus heifers.

The stockyards' 46 acres of sprawling pens, dusty alleys, and noisy sale rings are where, more than any other place in Sioux Falls, the city affirms its closeness to the agricultural economy that drives the rest of South Dakota. Before the stockyards began in 1917,

▲ 13-mile bike path winds along the Big Sioux River from the southwest side of the city through downtown to the falls. It's a rare and quiet moment when a photographer can snap an image that doesn't include bike riders, joggers, rollerbladers, or walkers.

area livestock was shipped, usually by rail, to Chicago, St. Paul, Minnesota, or Sioux City, Iowa. It cost farmers more and took business away from the area. When you learn that by 1982 the Sioux Falls Stockyards ranked first in the nation in overall sales, it helps you understand how much agriculture came to mean to the city.

Most of the working folks in the rest of the city are too busy getting kids off to school and themselves off to the job to ponder the rural-urban link the stockyards represent; the men and women of the yards don't worry much about philosophy, either. They move the steers or hogs or lambs where they're supposed to be, and then, if they have time, they head for the Stockyards Cafe for strong coffee and conversation.

If the stockyards symbolize the rural-urban spirit of Sioux Falls, nearby John Morrell & Co. represents the union of agriculture and industry, and the division of labor and management. Strikes, layoffs, cutbacks, and expansion make Morrell a regular part of South Dakota's evening news.

Morrell opened in 1909, and, even with a series of labor strikes and production cutbacks over the years, it continues to rank among the top five Sioux Falls employers. "There are some people who say Morrell really built Sioux Falls," says Roger Hainje, head of the Sioux Falls Economic Development Foundation.

As a former farm kid, I've always felt that the packing plant is much more than an employer or a job. It's a fascinating mix of steam and smells and noise stuffed into a hulking old building. We know what goes in and what comes out, but it's a mystery what goes on in the middle.

Back in high school, my Future Farmers of America club traveled to

Sioux Falls for livestock judging contests against kids from other schools. We'd hang on the fences at Morrell, studying beef on the hoof and trying to separate the canners and cutters from the choice to prime, pretending we didn't notice the muscled, swaggering meatcutters who ignored us as they moved from one task to another.

I suspect that Morrell will hold less fascination for future generations. Kids who grow up in the new Sioux Falls rather than on the farm are more likely to consider the place just a business. But to my generation and those before me, the stockyards and John Morrell are as much Sioux Falls as the cathedral and the old clock tower.

Up the hill from Morrell is another instantly recognizable piece of Sioux Falls. The South Dakota Penitentiary isn't something civic leaders brag about, but it's been an undeniable part of the city since 1882, an imposing hilltop presence with guard towers and thick granite walls. Its first major expansion, a new medium- and minimum-security wing for 288 inmates, is scheduled to open in early 1993.

When I was a kid visiting Sioux Falls, my sister and I would only whisper as we drove past the penitentiary. We would sit low in the car seats and never, ever look directly at the place, except in the rear window when we were safely past. I remembered those hushed trips the first time I was assigned to take photos inside the prison. I found it to be a noisy, mysterious place, and the memory of the way the strong, steel doors clanged shut still raises goose bumps.

Just over the hill from the penitentiary is the Sioux Falls airport, Joe Foss Field, a symbol both of how far into the modern world the city has moved and how close it remains to its past.

Named after the former governor and WWII flying ace, who also helped start the Air National Guard in 1946, the field is where I saw my first jet outside of the movies. In my case it was an F-86, the very model I'd seen in magnificent dogfights with Russian-built MiG-15s in films about the Korean War. The F-86 was the first in a long line of warplanes I've seen the South Dakota Air National Guard maintain and fly over the years.

Joe Foss Field is one of the reasons Sioux Falls sees more political candidates than other cities in the state. The biggest airplanes land here, including Air Force One, which most recently cruised to a landing in September 1992 so President George Bush could deliver a farm policy speech.

That reminds me, the first national presidential candidate I ever saw up close landed here. New York Senator Robert F. Kennedy was campaigning in the 1968 election. As he stepped from the plane, I was surprised at how frail he looked, short, thin, and tired. Backing up and shooting pictures, I managed somehow to step on the polished left shoe of CBS's Roger Mudd. "Enthusiastic crowd," he said. "Sorry, sir," I mumbled.

Of course, it isn't just the airfield that draws the politicians. With South Dakota's largest newspaper, three television stations, and one-seventh of the state's population, Sioux Falls is a must stop for the candidates.

Perhaps the most memorable national election for Sioux Falls was in 1972. That's because our own Democratic Senator George McGovern, a native of nearby Mitchell, South Dakota, was running against incumbent President Richard Nixon. McGovern set up election-night headquarters in the downtown Holiday Inn, and that meant the whole flying circus of staff, secret service, and reporters hit the city, too.

McGovern lost that election, and his late-evening appearance at a Coliseum rally was an unhappy affair. But his campaign allowed Sioux Falls to experience first-hand the carnival atmosphere that surrounds a presidential election night, and those who were even on the fringes of the event won't likely forget it.

That's sure to be one of the differences between older generations and up-and-coming Sioux Falls residents. Things like politicians jetting into the local airport aren't likely to be such a big deal. They'll have seen a dozen of the biggest names by the time they're my age.

No, if I were guessing, I'd say that when the next generation writes its chapter in the Sioux Falls story, the places that stand out will be far from the stockyards and John Morrell. It's likely that the next generation,

asked what says Sioux Falls to them, would instantly reply, "The Empire mall." If they were to be more general, they'd likely say, "41st Street."

And, why not? In 1991, South Dakota saw a total of $5.2 billion in taxable sales. Sioux Falls enjoyed $1.4 billion of that, more than 25 percent. A good share of that business occurs along Empire-anchored 41st Street. But retailing is only part of the reason the new generation will identify the mall with Sioux Falls. It's where the gang gathers these days.

In town for the tournaments? Time was, we'd have a soda at Lemond's or a pizza at Charlie's. Now we'll meet you at the mall. Back to school time? Let's hit Sioux Falls Saturday and shop. Want to catch Garth Brooks or Def Leppard or the latest rap group in concert? They'll be at the Arena. Let's kill some time at the mall first. Interested in hearing White Eagle, the Sioux Indian opera singer? He's appearing with the South Dakota Symphony. Why don't we make a day of it in the city?

I suspect, though, that malls and shops won't be the only way the new generation identifies Sioux Falls. I'm guessing Citibank South Dakota, the huge credit-card operation located in an industrial park north of the city, will be one of the city's future landmarks.

Citibank came to South Dakota in 1981, after then-Governor Bill Janklow

persuaded legislators to relax state limits on interest rates. In its first decade of business here the financial giant has grown to employ 2,800 people and to pay an estimated $30 million in state bank franchise taxes. A 1992 report showed only John Morrell & Co. provides more Sioux Falls jobs, 3,000.

When Citibank opened, the *Argus Leader* described the operation as "a new, weather-proof business for a state economy that lives and dies on rainfall." Those few simple words spoke volumes to residents of a state that knows dry-land farming.

Although the population of Sioux Falls has grown to more than 100,000, scenes such as these are seldom more distant than a few minutes' drive.

Another operation that should become a landmark in Sioux Falls' future is EROS, the Earth Resources Observation Systems Data Center, located near Garretson just north of the city. Established in 1971, EROS is a place where satellite pictures of the earth are received and interpreted. The importance of that science to agriculture is only beginning to be appreciated, but the presence of the space-age technology just a few miles from the 70-year-old stockyards illustrates that a historian was right when he said South Dakota was a place where the frontier and the edge of space are still incredibly close together.

How Sioux Falls landed EROS says something about the city's continuing drive and foresight. The Sioux Falls Economic Development Foundation raised $240,000 to buy 320 acres of land for the center, and when the government didn't have money set aside for construction, the foundation helped finance that, too. The result was about

350 high-tech jobs and the families who came with those workers.

Well, I could speculate forever about future landmarks. Let's hop around town and see some sights I know will continue to be big in the city. What do you say we start at the zoo?

The Great Plains Zoo, just off Kiwanis Avenue south of 12th Street, has been here since 1963. That's about the time neighbors started waking to the patter of tiny feet on the roof. Every so often a monkey escapes, you see. Most folks are just glad is isn't the panther. People who know the history

Dawn is reflected in the glass walls of a modern downtown office building as a new day draws hundreds of workers to the city's center.

of the zoo claim that in the early days the lions wintered over in Terrace Park in a garage belonging to a descendent of J.L. Phillips. Today's 32-acre site is home to 72 species and over 240 animals.

This is not the first zoo in Sioux Falls, according to historians Gary and Erik Olson. No less a city father than R.F. Pettigrew founded a zoo in the late 1800s, featuring buffalo, elk, and, well, prairie dogs. It didn't last, though. The last buffalo was sold to Buffalo, New York, in 1894.

Next door to the zoo is an off-beat treasure, the wild animal collection of Henry Brockhouse in the Delbridge Museum of Natural History. The long-time hardware store owner was nuts about big-game hunting. He displayed his success—stuffed, mounted ele-

phants, rhinos, and tigers—in his store for years. When he died in 1980, the city inherited the collection, with the condition that the animals be displayed.

Right next to the Delbridge Museum is Sherman Park. It's the place where the ancient Indian burial mounds were found, remember? If that glimpse of Native American culture whets your appetite, you can learn more about the first inhabitants of this area from the Sioux Indian collection at the Pettigrew Home and Museum. The Civic Fine Arts Center also frequently includes the creations of Native American artists among its displays; most recently, the works of Oscar Howe, a South Dakota Sioux, were featured. And a broad selection of Native American artwork is on display and sale at the annual Northern Plains Tribal Arts show, hosted every September since 1988 by the American Indian Service.

Don't leave Sherman Park, though, until you've seen the memorial to the USS Battleship *South Dakota*, the most decorated American warship of World War II. Several pieces of the battleship, scrapped in 1960, were salvaged and included in the memorial, which features a concrete, battleship-size silhouette, as well as the Tiffany silver service presented to the captain on the first voyage in 1942. You won't see an entire vessel here, but you'll get an idea of the size of one of these fighting ships. You'll also get a sense of the commitment to the nation that's always been a part of the Sioux Falls spirit.

West of the park across Interstate 29 is a part of town that used to be

identified with old Hayward Elementary School. The school is gone now, closed in 1986 and torn down four years later after a gasoline spill from nearby Williams Pipe Line Co. was discovered.

More than 20,000 gallons of gasoline leaked into the ground from the pipeline company's property, forcing Hayward to be closed and its students shipped to schools throughout the rest of the city. Property values plummeted for a time, and many homeowners feared they'd hit bottom. But the spill was cleaned, a new school (that kids naturally call New Hayward) was built not far away, and the area rebounded. Since 1980, 150 new homes have gone up in the neighborhood.

The speed with which Sioux Falls responded to the Hayward emergency is just one example of the city's commitment to community and education. Other examples are springing up all over town. There's the new Washington High school, which opened in the fall of 1992 on the east side of town, replacing the storied but worn-out downtown fortress that produced more than 30,000 alumni. There's Roosevelt High, which opened in 1991 in the middle of the westside growth area. Before that there was Lincoln High and John Harris Elementary. The new buildings have just kept on coming.

While much of South Dakota wrestles with ways to keep school systems operating for fewer and fewer students, Sioux Falls struggles to keep up with the growth that's adding 450 or more students a year to the public system. "We'll manage, too," says retired Superintendent John Harris. "This is one community that, when it complains to the school board or administration, generally talks about the need for more programs, not cuts. Good education is an important concern here."

On a hillside just southeast of Sherman Park's forest, the Royal C. Johnson Veterans Memorial Hospital offers medical care to the area's active and retired soldiers. Sioux Falls first opened a hospital for veterans in a downtown location after World War I. The current building, completed in 1949, is an imposing structure, four stories high with a center tower and wings that sweep away on each side. An immaculately kept lawn drops away from the front drive, a huge tract of grass where kids fly kites and throw baseballs.

I encountered some of the most amazing characters of my journalistic career in the VA hospital. Even a cub photographer could see the portrait possibilities in the deeply lined faces of the patients. One old gentleman, who told me his leg had never recovered from a German bullet he'd taken in France in World War I, seemed to have a sixth sense about when a photo shoot was scheduled. He was always there to meet me—in the hall, near the front door, somewhere. He didn't want to talk about the war or himself; he just pumped me for the latest on my job, my home, my baby girl. He never told me his name, and he always called me "Sonny." The cracked tile of the hallway would groan under our feet as we walked back toward his room, and he'd put a bony hand on my forearm if I moved too quickly. "I got all day, Sonny," he'd say.

The low-roofed complex with the distinctive Spanish design just across the street from the VA is the Park Ridge Shopping Mall. It was developed in 1955, the first mall in town. Dale Skadsen started a shoe repair business there when Park Ridge opened. I took a pair of shoes there in 1967, and I could take another pair there today. There's a permanence to this neighborhood mall nobody could have predicted when it began.

When Richard Bielski bought the two blocks along Western Avenue and started Park Ridge, a lot of folks chuckled. This was backcountry in those days, and few residents foresaw how quickly the growing city would surround them. The whole area, with its narrow streets, comfortable ranch-style homes, and shady ash and maple trees, developed during the business and baby boom following the WWII. It has been one of the most stable residential areas in the city, and children from today's neighborhood go to Jefferson Elementary School or nearby Christ the King Catholic School, just as their parents did a generation earlier.

Not far to the north, the University of South Dakota Medical School is one of the newest additions to the area. For decades South Dakota operated a two-year medical school at the University of South Dakota in Vermillion. Students

were forced to transfer to medical colleges in other states to complete their education, and they often remained in those states to perform residencies and set up practices.

The 1974 legislature wanted to keep more doctors in the state, so it approved a degree-granting medical school at USD. The heart of the operation has slowly moved from Vermillion to Sioux Falls, drawn by the growing medical community and the fact that many of the early USD graduates established their practices in the city. In 1991, Sioux Valley Hospital

▶ KIRBY SCHULTZ

The whimsical notion of a violin with strings of wheat stalks illustrates the way culture and country intertwine in southeastern South Dakota.

donated $6 million for construction of a permanent headquarters for the USD medical school. The site will be in the hospital neighborhood.

To the southwest, National College, a regionally recognized business school, is located near O'Gorman High School, which is a private Catholic school located, complete with playing fields, smack in the midst of all the 41st Street commercial development.

The Central Plains Clinic almost touches O'Gorman's pale brick buildings. Since the clinic moved to the area in 1976—searching for a spot with room to grow—it has done just that, expanding to accommodate more than 80 doctors. It's considered the largest medical clinic in the state, and now does business on three sites in various parts of Sioux Falls, headquartering

near McKennan Hospital. Not bad for a place that started in 1921 as a small band of doctors in an office building on Minnesota Avenue.

Ever since the Western Mall opened down the street in 1968, Sioux Falls people have called this part of town the "mall area." And, with what are probably the richest pieces of commercial real estate in South Dakota within its boundaries, it's true that this is the heart of retailing for the entire state. The Empire mall, for example, welcomes 10 million to 12 million people a year.

When the Western Mall opened in 1968, it seemed an amazing thing to be able to park in a huge, open lot—with no parking meters to feed—enter one door and walk and shop two or three blocks of stores without ever considering the weather or wondering if there would be a bench nearby to rest your aching feet. It was too easy.

Not long ago an editorial in the *Argus Leader* suggested that the city's reaction to the Western Mall opening is one reason Sioux Falls has continued to grow. "The city never fought the movement of retailing to the 41st Street corridor," the paper said. "Sioux City [Iowa] took the opposite course, forcing stores to stay downtown. By the time a shopping center finally was built in Sioux City, Sioux Falls had a lock on shoppers in the southeastern part of South Dakota as well as adjoining Iowa, Minnesota, and Nebraska."

Sioux Falls made a strong commitment to retailing by its decision. It also made a strong commitment to the things that support business and economic growth—like recreation. Beautiful McKennan Park, just a five-minute drive from the heart of downtown, is only one of 50 city parks in the developing park system. Helen Gale McKennan gave the land for the park to the city in 1906. In the years since, it has become one of Sioux Falls' true landmarks.

Located a short walk south of downtown, the park was quickly encircled by grand two- and three-story houses, so that today it's a seamless continuation of towering shade trees and elegant homes.

McKennan's tennis courts host area high school and college matches on fall and spring weekends, and in the summer the courts swarm with youngsters just beginning to learn the difference between a ground stroke and an overhead smash.

Another sign of the city's commitment to recreation is the bicycle trail that winds along the Big Sioux River. The 13 miles of pavement start at Falls Park, but you can pedal, stroll, or jog onto the trail at any number of entrances as it loops lazily south to 41st Street, west almost to Interstate 29, and then north to the airport.

As you explore the trail, you're sure to pass close to one of the Lewis Drug Stores. Started by a trio headed by the late John Griffin in 1942, they're a special part of Sioux Falls' business heritage. He enlarged upon an odd new notion that people should be able to serve themselves. Up to that time, a drugstore was a place where you went to the counter and waited while a clerk gathered your order for you. In Lewis stores, beginning with the one downtown on Phillips Avenue, you could just wander around the store, choosing items one by one, then settle up at the cash register when you were finished. A remarkable idea.

If you travel the part of the bike path that skirts the eastern edge of downtown, you're sure to pass near Fawick Park and the statue of *David*, a gift to the city that nearly tore Sioux Falls apart. That's a story that tells a lot about the delicate equilibrium between artistic freedom and prairie prudishness that exists among Sioux Falls residents.

Fawick Park is named for Thomas Fawick, who grew up in Sioux Falls in the early 1900s. Young Tom dropped out of school at age 14, but by the time he was 18, he'd designed and built an automobile, the Fawick Flyer. The first Flyer, a four-cylinder job, never sold, but there's one on display today at the Old Courthouse Museum. A local doctor bought a later model of the Flyer, one of the first cars with four doors, and President Teddy Roosevelt rode in that car during a 1910 visit to town.

Eventually, the enterprising Fawick sought his fortune elsewhere, building a $42 million business from a variety of mechanical inventions. When Augustana College gave him an honorary degree in 1971, he generously responded with a gift to the city of a replica of Michelangelo's *David*, considered one of the heights of achievement in Western art. Did that cause problems.

David, local citizens soon discovered, was more than triple life-sized and entirely naked to boot. Well, after a good deal of hearty debate, the somewhat-grateful city decided to accept the statue and place it in lovely Fawick Park, next to the 10th Street viaduct—but only after it was assured *David* would be facing away from the heavily traveled streets nearby.

Sioux Falls may have been a bit hesitant about its public art, but there was precedent for the attitude. After all, even a big town like Chicago pooh-poohed the huge Picasso sculp-

▶ ROD JONES

Outlined against a blue-black sky, Michelangelo's *David* greets visitors to Fawick Park, just a stroll from downtown Sioux Falls.

ture when it was erected in 1967. In Fresno, the Alexander Calder inspired cackles and bewilderment from its citizens. So if Sioux Falls was a bit cautious, it's no less committed to the growth of the fine and performing arts.

For instance, there are local theater productions regularly at the Sioux Falls Community Playhouse, the Olde Towne Theatre in nearby Worthing, the Barn Theater near Tea, and both Augustana College and Sioux Falls College.

If classic music productions are more to your taste, there are seasonal performances by the South Dakota Symphony, under the direction of Henry Charles Smith. In 1992, soloists from the New York Grand Opera were scheduled to sing with the symphony. The city also boasts the Sioux Falls

Master Singers, a chorus that offers several concerts each year. The Friends of Traditional Music, which brings in bluegrass, folk, and related types of music, appears at locations all across the community, and the Community Concert Association, an annual program of visiting artists and groups, schedules its performances at the Coliseum.

I told you an early Fawick Flyer was on display at the Old Courthouse Museum. That's one of a variety of museums where you can find interesting exhibits. Augustana College's Center for Western Studies is another. The Civic Fine Arts Center offers changing shows of local and national artists; the Pettigrew Home and Museum includes pioneer artifacts and natural history exhibits, as well as Sioux Indian displays; the Sioux Empire Medical Museum at Sioux Valley Hospital specializes in medical history; and the Berdahl-Rolvaag House on the campus at Augustana gives a glimpse of prairie life in the restored home of the wife of Ole Rolvaag, who told the story of early South Dakota in his novel *Giants in the Earth*.

Well, those are some of the sights and events you'll want to experience when you're in the city. I could show you many other things of historical note and cultural note and, probably, some plain old Sioux Falls eccentricities, but you can find most of them yourself. Just start in any direction. It's an easy city to travel through, and, if you get lost, pull over and ask the guy raking his leaves for help. The people are still small-town friendly here.

I'm going back along the bike trail to Falls Park now. That's where we started this story, and that's where I think I'll leave you. I want to sit by the falls for a bit. Plans are in the works to renovate this entire area, both to make it more attractive for visitors and to make more people realize the significance of the river and the falls in the history, growth, and future of Sioux Falls.

Why, right now as I'm sitting here, there are people over by the old Queen Bee Mill kicking off a restoration drive.

Now, that's the spirit.

SITTING HERE BY THE FALLS, I'M TEMPTED TO SHUCK my shoes and socks and leap along the rocks worn flat and slippery by the swollen river during its annual spring flow. I can almost hear my mother, "Don't you dare, young man!" The same warning, I suppose, that generations of children have heard from their mothers. ◆ It occurs to me that the falls of the Big Sioux River are one place in

the city where the past and future meet. Like the rest of South Dakota, Sioux Falls is a young place, compared with much of the nation. John Milton, the USD historian, wrote in his 1976 bicentennial book that those of us who live here on the plains may be unique: "Never before in history has man stood

TIM STEINBERG

Few sights are more majestic than the falls of the Big Sioux River when the water booms against the rock and foams in deep pools. The pedestrian bridge at Falls Park is an ideal place to see and hear the power of this natural wonder.

with one foot in his primitive origins and the other poised on the moon."

That's how I feel about the falls, particularly as I sit here and watch the water swirl, plunge, and foam. This place is a constant.

Drop J.L. Phillips down at the intersection of 41st Street and Kiwanis Avenue today and even a man with his foresight could hardly comprehend the changes of the past century. Put him here by the falls on a quiet evening, though, and he'd have to look closely to see anything different from his first visit to the place.

I'd like to think that the same might be true for me if I were able to return in, say, 50 years. In that time, I know much of Sioux Falls will have grown and changed beyond my comprehension. I suspect I'd still recognize the falls. It will be one of my enduring memories.

So will such purely Sioux Falls places, characters, and experiences as:

◆ The voice of the Sioux Falls Stockyards, Les Harding, who brought the cattle, sheep, and hog markets to the country each day.

◆ The jumbo highballs at the old Stockman's Bar, where workers used to gather after the stockyards shut down and the shift changed at John Morrell.

◆ Captain 11 watching the needles on the time converter flicker as he prepared to show a cartoon. The Dave Dedrick character has been a part of children's television in the city since 1955.

◆ Rich Greeno in sweatshirt and stocking cap, grinning as he loped along during a practice run with members of his always-in-contention Lincoln High School cross-country team.

◆ The gas wars in the 1960s, with people waiting to get into Ripco on East 10th for a fill at 19 cents a gallon.

◆ The clean smell of just-clipped outfield grass and the yell of the guy selling popcorn just about sundown when the Sioux Falls Packers were opening a Northern League home stand.

◆ The zaniness that overcame the city every March 17 when green shamrocks adorned the downtown streets for the annual St. Patrick's Day parade. In snowstorms and rain showers, the Irish and would-be Irish still turn out each year to make sure Sioux Falls has the biggest St. Pat's celebration in the state.

◆ The new Sioux Falls Post Office, completed in 1966, just in time for a generation of young men to report for draft physicals and induction into the U.S. Army.

◆ The first obituary a young reporter really paid attention to. When former Mayor V.L. Crusinberry died on December 12, 1967, the lead paragraph said simply but eloquently, "The big

man with the long name is dead."

◆ The dramatic, prize-winning 1967 photograph by Ray Mews, shooting at the time for the *Argus Leader*. Mews captured, in stark black-and-white, the moment a wounded South Dakota soldier returned from Vietnam to the tight embrace of his wife. The amputee's wooden crutch, lying on the runway where it was dropped in the fierce reunion, said more than any cutline could have.

◆ The old *Argus Leader* building with the sidewalk window where kids could stand and watch the presses run.

◆ Mr. Bendo, the big, bearded guy holding the section of tailpipe by the muffler shop on South Cliff Avenue.

◆ The hum of tires rolling over the steel mesh deck of the Cherry Rock bridge.

◆ The sight of thousands of people moving along Phillips Avenue during the Sidewalk Arts Festival.

◆ The weatherball blinking atop the downtown First Bank of South Dakota building, a sure sign of precipitation to come.

No one person can describe all of Sioux Falls. It's too many things to too many people. I have a friend who loves the city as much as I do, though, and he does a pretty good job of expressing what it means to him. I'll leave you with his thoughts.

Dave Munson grew up in the North End neighborhoods, played baseball in the streets, and rode Christmas sleds down the hills near the cathedral. He taught school and coached, won a seat in the state House of Representatives, and became an officer at Citibank.

"When I was growing up, we didn't think about race, unemployment, politics, or finances, we just thought about the other kids in the neighborhood," Munson says. "After school we'd grab our bats and gloves or go shoot baskets. Somebody's mom or dad always knew where we were. It was a feeling like the whole neighborhood was part of a big family. Sioux Falls has grown an incredible amount since then, but I still get that feeling that we all care about each other. That's the one thing I'd never want to see change about the community."

What he's describing is spirit, the spirit of Sioux Falls.

For more than a century, youngsters in Sioux Falls have received their first lessons in rock climbing on the rough granite walls of the city's namesake.

A hot summer afternoon and a tempting pool of cool Big Sioux River water—what kid can resist that combination?

Following pages: The skeleton of an old mill bears stark witness to one of many failed efforts by pioneering entrepreneurs to harness the energy of the falls.
Rod Jones photo

29

The stone remains of the old Queen Bee Mill, one of the first structures in Sioux Falls, continue to be a popular natural playground for area youngsters. The abundance of quartzite deposits around the falls made the stone one of the basic building blocks of the early city.

The clock tower of the Old County Courthouse (top) can be seen from every direction in the city. Built in 1889, the courthouse is now home to the Siouxland Heritage Museum.

(Bottom) When folks said "high school" in Sioux Falls, they meant Washington High, the downtown brick fortress that served all the city until Lincoln High opened in 1965. The last class at old Washington High graduated in 1992.

The Japanese Gardens near Terrace
Park offer a touch of oriental serenity
in the heart of a thriving western city.

Modern glass-sided buildings coexist with comfortable old brick stores in the downtown business district.

A century of change is reflected in the windows of an office building. The old and the new mix in Sioux Falls in a graphic illustration of how truly close to its roots the city remains.

The glass front of the Midland National Life building captures a perfect summer day.

You wouldn't expect an architect to have a plain, old office front, and the building housing the firm started by Harold Spitznagel in the 1930s doesn't disappoint.

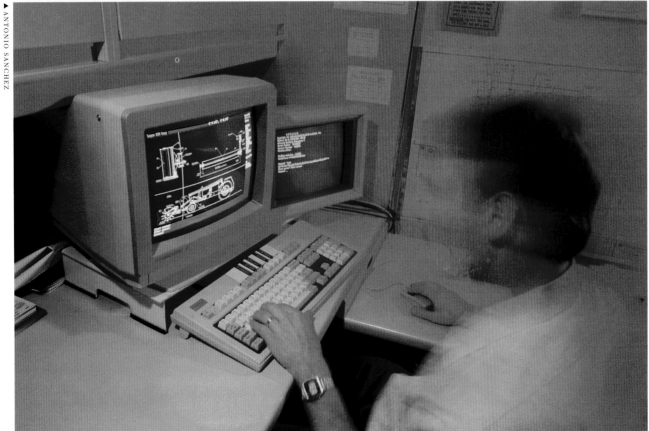

The computer age really came to South Dakota in 1971, when Sioux Falls won the competition as the site for EROS (Earth Resources Observation Systems) Data Center (top).

Since then, computers have become commonplace in the office setting.

Always a state leader in economic growth, Sioux Falls has been aggressive in seeking and wooing manufacturing businesses that keep jobs and people flowing into the city.

THE BUS STOP

The evening rush from the downtown area is nearly finished, and the quiet streets give the city the feel of a small-town Saturday night (above).

A lantern shines in the early morning shadows near the train station as a Burlington Northern freight is being prepared for the day's run (opposite).

The maze of pens and alleys at the Sioux Falls Stockyards takes on a sensible order when seen from one of the high catwalks that span the livestock area. The stockyards have grown from a small outlet for area farmers to one of the busiest in the nation.

Long before the sun rises, the coffee's on and the talk is loud at the Stockyards Cafe (top). In recent years, the stock-yards have sold as many hogs as any market in the nation (bottom).

Workers from nearby John Morrell & Co. and drivers and cattle buyers from the stockyards once gathered after hours at the Stockman's Bar, where the size of the hi-balls rated mention in neon lights (opposite).

With a century of growth, it's inevitable that the city would become home to many of the state's homeless and needy. In a city of churches, this stucco-sided mission is one more sign of hope for those needing help (above).

The soaring ceilings and stained glass windows of St. Joseph's Cathedral are familiar to Roman Catholics throughout the diocese of Sioux Falls.

The cathedral is the heart of a neighborhood of magnificent old homes just west of the downtown area.

A statue of Joseph with the Christ child is framed by the towering facade of the cathedral, which was built in 1917. It replaced St. Michael's Catholic Church, built in 1883, one of the original churches constructed during Sioux Falls' early boom years.

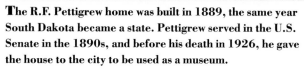

The R.F. Pettigrew home was built in 1889, the same year South Dakota became a state. Pettigrew served in the U.S. Senate in the 1890s, and before his death in 1926, he gave the house to the city to be used as a museum.

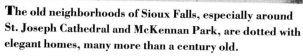

The old neighborhoods of Sioux Falls, especially around
St. Joseph Cathedral and McKennan Park, are dotted with
elegant homes, many more than a century old.

▼ LLOYD CUNNINGHAM

Lowell Voight's collection of World War II records and early radios and phonographs reflects an appreciation of a turbulent era and a love for the early inventions that changed the way we all communicate.

Sioux Falls' array of medical services, shops, parks, and activities prompts many people of retirement age, like Ralph and Ruth Morris (top), to spend their senior years in the city.

From proven performers to untried amateurs, there's no limit to the variety of music that can be found in Sioux Falls. Myron Floren (top right), a South Dakota native showcased for years with the Lawrence Welk orchestra, returns on a regular basis to give concerts with his own band.

The polkas and waltzes Floren's accordion pumps out are a different rhythm from the modern moves the younger set favors (bottom right). The Sioux Falls Symphony (top, bottom left) brings a more classical feeling to the music scene with its annual series of performances and guest artists.

54

Sioux Falls appreciates down-home music, as practiced by old-time fiddle king Wilbur Foss (top left) of Yankton and enjoyed by a country couple at a local dance hall (bottom left). And there's always time for a few tunes from the old country as played by the

Scottish bagpiper, part of a group from Winnipeg, Canada, that travels south each March 17 to be part of the St. Patrick's Day parade.

The St. Patrick's Day parade is an annual bit of March madness in downtown Sioux Falls, with huge green shamrocks painted on the pavement and floats like the one above featuring just about everyone in South Dakota whose last name is Garry. The parade is always a traffic stopper, as Police Officer Mike Milstead (top opposite) shows. Eager junior traffic guards (bottom opposite) work on their techniques.

Opportunities for stimulating young minds abound, whether in a classroom setting or on field trips. Part of the excitement of having the Great Plains Zoo in the community comes from informal "show and tell" sessions with area school children.

▲ TIM STEINBERG

▲ JOEL STRASSER

The Great Plains Zoo opened its doors in 1963, and a refurbished entrance (top) was completed in 1984. The Delbridge Museum of Natural History (bottom) displays animals hunted by the late big-game enthusiast and hardware store owner Henry Brockhouse.

Following pages: The big cats at the zoo always send delicious chills down the spines of young visitors.
The Argus Leader photo

Less immediately threatening are the bears. Housed in an area very much like their natural habitat, they often seem oblivious to the hundreds of spectators who crowd the observation decks.
Ken Starkenburg photo

59

A falcon appears to be staring down the photographer at the bird houses of the Great Plains Zoo (opposite).

The wild blue yonder looks doubly wild over Sioux Falls on summer days when thunderheads climb the sky to darken the sun (top).

On the ground, members of South Dakota's Air National Guard prepare for a training flight (bottom).

The action is furious all over Sioux Falls in the summer, whether it's college or high school baseball or the rodeo. A South Dakota cowboy (top right) tries to keep his seat for eight seconds atop a whirling brahma bull, while a cowgirl leans to help her horse around the turn in barrel racing (bottom right).

MIKE ROEMER

TIM STEINBERG

Summer is a time for less formal sports, too, such as skateboarding in a city park, water skiing at Wall Lake, tube riding at Wild Water West amusement park, or splashing in the shallow water at the edge of the Big Sioux River.

Local businessman Dick Kelley, who entertains as Squeezer the Clown, gets an appreciative reception from a small fan.

A late summer highlight in the Sioux Falls area is the week-long Sioux Empire Fair, a celebration of crafts and hobbies, carnival rides, music shows, and auto races.

Card games have always helped pass a long Midwest evening. The setting (top) is less formal than at the Royal River Casino in Flandreau (bottom), but the concentration of the players is no less fierce.

Sheriff Les Hawkey enforces the law in Minnehaha County, and his responsibility continues to grow. The county's population reached 123,809 in 1990, up from 109,435 in the previous U.S. census.

Pastor Mack Henderson of the Pentecostal Temple is part of a strong community of faith in Sioux Falls.

Organized religion in a variety of denominations and ministries has long been a part of the fabric of the Sioux Falls community. Some of the earliest visitors were priests and ministers who traveled with the first explorers. Even before that, the Native American tribes that inhabited the area had their own spiritual values and customs.

The falls of the Big Sioux River were home to Indian tribes centuries before white settlers arrived, and the Native American tradition is still celebrated and reinforced in annual powwows. The traditional Indian costumes become a brilliant blur of color as the dancers whirl and dip.

Following pages: In a land of clean air and transparent skies, rainbows sometimes seem to reach forever, especially when they're built by the setting sun after a summer afternoon shower. These arching rainbows seem to reach from the country church to the field of deep-green corn.
Ken Starkenburg photo, page 72
Joel Strasser photo, page 73

Indians used to tie young trees down so the trunks would grow crooked. It was the old way of marking a water source. This aged cottonwood tree grows along the White River south of Interior, South Dakota in Badlands National Park.

▼ TIM STEINBERG

▼ TIM STEINBERG

▼ JOEL STRASSER

▼ JOEL STRASSER

Each South Dakota season brings a unique look and feel to the land, a welcome and valued sense of change and renewal.

PAUL BUCKOWSKI

JOEL STRASSER

JOEL STRASSER

JOEL STRASSER

Sioux Falls educates more students from kindergarten through college than any other city in the state. When the trees are blossoming on a warm spring afternoon, however, that fact is probably far from the minds of a couple walking between classes at Augustana College (opposite).

A ripening cherry is covered with ice crystals from a surprise cold snap (top). Most of the time, the growing season is pretty predictable, and roses thrive in the summer warmth (bottom).

Seen from above, a field of beans in Minnehaha County farm country looks like the product of the weaver's shuttle rather than the plow (opposite).

South Dakotans thought balloons were decorations for birthday parties until Raven Industries hit town and began making industrial-size balloons for industry and the military. In recent years the city has been home to a host of hot-air balloon enthusiasts, many of whom fly colorfully decorated models like this one of Old Glory floating above a township highway.

Preceding pages: The Big Sioux isn't all rushing rapids and falls. For long stretches it wanders peacefully between banks covered with cottonwood trees. A guitarist finds a quiet place by the river to practice a new song.
Two youngsters seem to be having a successful fishing trip.
Mike Roemer photo, page 80
Paul Buckowski photo, page 81

No matter how much the city grows, Sioux Falls is never far from its rural roots. Area farmers let their horse graze while they exchange opinions on chances for an evening rain (above).

The eastern border counties in South Dakota are home to the bulk of the state's thriving dairy industry (opposite).

JOEL STRASSER

JOEL STRASSER

White-faced Herefords, with their
red-tinged hides, are a popular breed
for cattle feeders in Minnehaha County.

Within a few minutes' drive of downtown Sioux Falls, the adventuresome can find an isolated stretch of meadow for a soothing horseback ride, a popular sport and necessary skill on the prairie.

Winter has come and gone on the farm, (opposite) but this snow fence leans in memory of the weight of a drift.

Old but reliable is the way some county farmers would describe well-used equipment. Many country kids got their first lessons in field work on an old tractor outfitted with a mower and side-rake, much like the one in the top photograph.

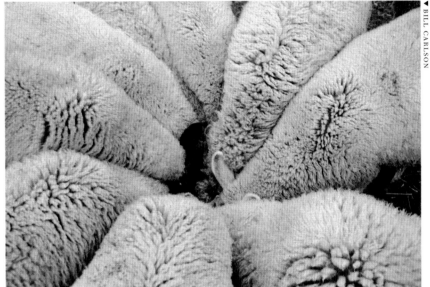

Farm country offers a variety of patterns and textures, ranging from the weathered siding on an old barn (left) to the peeling spokes of a wagon wheel (top). Hungry sheep circle and squeeze together at the feed bucket (bottom).

Following pages: The Minnehaha County countryside around Sioux Falls contains some of the richest farmland in the region. Whether showing off a bumper corn crop waiting to be harvested or filling a pot with homegrown vegetables at one of the numerous summer celebrations of rural life, folks clearly recognize agriculture's importance in the Sioux Falls story.
Lloyd Cunningham photos

The late Gordon Olson, shown working
at his backyard grill, was a tireless
promoter of the city as a Sioux Falls
Area Chamber of Commerce executive.

Opportunities for fine dining in Sioux Falls range from the down-home variety (top) to the elegant ambience of one of dozens of restaurants (bottom).

Sometimes it seems the city hasn't moved very far from the farm at all, although an old-fashioned threshing machine is a novelty these days and not a necessity at harvest time.

The growing city pushes its boundaries farther and farther into the country, and homebuilders scurry to keep up with the demands of new families for suburban shelter.

Following pages: September sunlight fashioning shadows from the rafters of a new house is a common sight around Sioux Falls. With the city growing at the rate of 600 people every three months, the construction industry is never completely idle.
Tim Steinberg photo

Heavy steel girders and hot rivets are a constant around town. New stores, expanding factories, and office buildings are springing up at nearly the same rate as new houses.
Paul Buckowski photo

JOEL STRASSER

JOEL STRASSER

Sioux Falls has always been in the forefront of new ideas in design and construction as shown by these views of St. Mark's Lutheran Church (top) and St. Michael's Catholic Church (bottom).

98

Many of the city's new homes, especially in the southern growth areas, have been designed and built with an eye-catching flair and a modern appreciation for natural light and spaciousness.

In Sioux Falls, the quality of emergency care contributes to the community's reputation for excellence, as demonstrated by advances in helicopter ambulance service and 911 emergency response facilities.

Shadows play against the thick smoke as a Sioux Falls firefighter moves toward a blaze (left). The Central Fire Station at 9th and Minnesota (right) has been in operation since the late 1910s.

Sioux Falls fire fighters have battled a number of spectacular blazes in the downtown area in recent years . Local businesses are quick to clean up and rebuild, demonstrating a faith in the stability and future of their city.

Although most South Dakotans link mining activity with the gold mines of the Black Hills, Sioux Falls is the hub for an active gravel and quartzite mining industry.

Folks in Minnehaha County's farm country display autumn's melons, gourds, and corn at roadside stands (top). What would autumn be without the thrill of a Halloween trick-or-treat outing (bottom)?

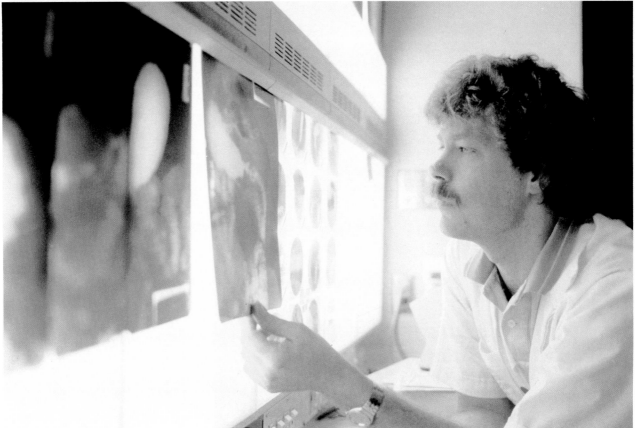

The growth of both McKennan and Sioux Valley hospitals, along with the presence of the University of South Dakota Medical School's offices, has propelled Sioux Falls to the forefront as a regional center for medical care, research, and education.

Huset's Speedway has been packing in the fans for years to enjoy some of the best auto racing in the region. Flagman Doug Clarke is a fixture at the track.

Augustana College was founded in 1918 on the site of the former Lutheran Normal School, which traces its beginnings to 1889. Augie's football Vikings play their home games at Howard Wood Field.

▲ BILL GOEHRING, MEDIA ONE INC.

▲ MIKE ROEMER

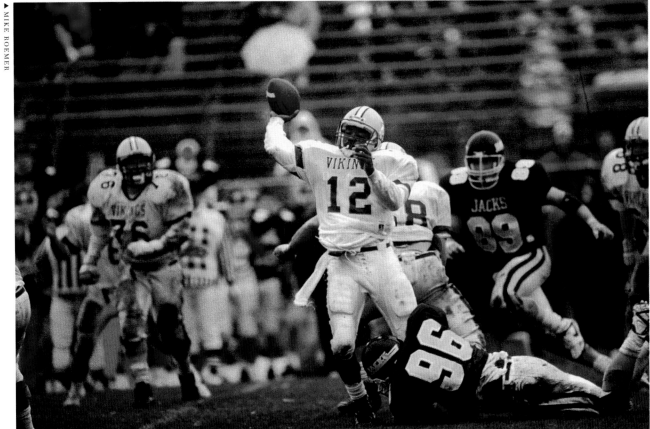

Members of the Augustana Vikings offense gather on the sidelines for a pre-game strategy session (top). The Vikings play NCAA Division II football in the North Central Conference, which each year produces at least two Top 20 teams. The annual rivalry is fierce between the Vikings and the South Dakota State University Jackrabbits (bottom).

A young violinist in the pit orchestra listens to the director's suggestions during rehearsal for a production of the Sioux Falls Community Playhouse. The popular community theater offers variety in its annual playbill, ranging from classics such as Shakespeare's *The Tempest* (top right) to the recent *Driving Miss Daisy.*

A flair for the dramatic is evident in recent stagings at the Sioux Falls Community Playhouse, including *Into the Woods* (top left) and *Evita* (bottom left).

South Dakota natives, those from Sioux Falls included, say that one thing that keeps them in this part of the country is the variety of the seasons.

These two farm scenes illustrate what a difference six months can make, from the warm greens and browns of early fall to the crystal whiteness of late winter.

The folks who settled Sioux Falls were of hardy Norwegian, German, and Irish stock and considered cold winter days just another opportunity to enjoy the outdoors. Cross-country skiing (above) has become a popular snow sport, while (opposite) the city-owned Great Bear ski area offers hot doggers a chance to show their stuff.

Christmas doesn't always mean a blanket of soft snow, but for many area residents it means a trip to one of the tree farms, such as Bill Keiser's (above), to pick out just the right tree for the holidays.

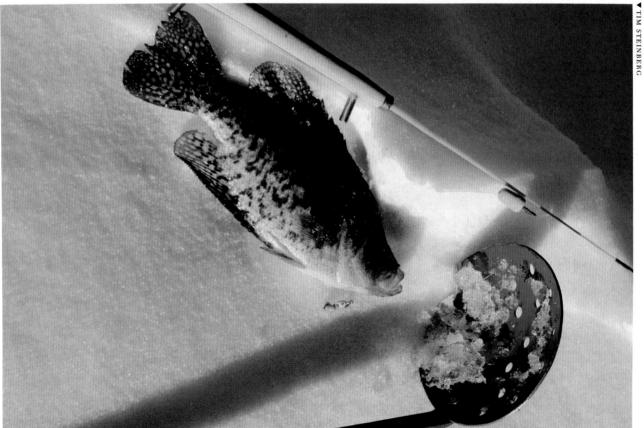

When the lakes freeze over for the winter, it doesn't take much gear to outfit an ice fishing trip. Heavy boots, a thick parka, and an overturned bucket beside a hole in the ice—combined with a bit of patience and luck—usually result in at least one or two catches.

In mid-winter, some of the lakes freeze hard enough to let fishermen drive right to their favorite spots, and before long, a mess of fillets are sizzling in the pan.

Although the average snowfall in Sioux Falls is 39.5 inches, the winter of 1968-69 brought almost 100 inches of the white stuff. Residents are pretty accustomed to the snow, however. When it falls, they shovel it, and go about their business.

A snow blower makes short work of clearing the sidewalk in front of a Sioux Falls business.

Following pages: Some days in a South Dakota winter, the air is so crisp it burns the lungs and the sky so pale it would disappear without the wisps of clouds hanging above the horizon.
Dan Jensen photo

Winter never freezes the falls, but it
fashions all sorts of ice sculptures over
the rocks. The early morning steam
turns to a thick fog that hides the upper
reaches of the river.

A completely different mood is set at the falls on a mild summer morning. The water foams as it pounds over the quartzite, and the shadows of the thickly leaved trees surround a visitor in a warm, reverie-inducing calm.

Following pages: Sioux Falls is a city of beautiful parks, more than 50 at last count. This couple enjoys a private moment at the end of the day.
Dan Jensen photo

SPIRIT OF

SIOUX FALLS

PROFILES IN EXCELLENCE

A LOOK AT THE CORPORATIONS, BUSINESSES,
PROFESSIONAL GROUPS, AND COMMUNITY SERVICE
ORGANIZATIONS THAT HAVE MADE THIS BOOK POSSIBLE.

By Stephen and Catherine Thurman

A century of change is evident in this
view of Phillips Avenue in downtown
Sioux Falls around 1888.

1878

Boyce, Murphy, McDowell
& Greenfield

1883

Sioux Falls College

1885

The First National Bank in
Sioux Falls

1887

Woods, Fuller,
Shultz & Smith, P.C.

1894

Sioux Valley Hospital

1907

Sioux Falls Area
Chamber of Commerce

1909

John Morrell & Co.

1910

Sioux Falls
Construction Company

1911

McKennan Hospital

1911

Parker Transfer
& Storage

THE OLDEST CONTINUOUSLY PRACTICING LAW FIRM IN Sioux Falls, Boyce, Murphy, McDowell & Greenfield was created in 1878 when Frank L. Boyce moved to Sioux Falls from Chicago and opened a law office. The lawyer had earlier visited Sioux Falls and, according to George Kingsbury's *History of South Dakota,* "Mr. Boyce was so well pleased with Dakota and so impressed with its future

possibilities that he concluded to make this city his future home."

When Boyce moved to Sioux Falls, the city was just beginning to experience the boom that would make it the "Queen City of the Dakotas." At the time of Boyce's arrival, Sioux Falls boasted a downtown of just one street, Phillips Avenue, which was lined with one- and two-story frame buildings with false fronts. Sioux Falls was a city to grow in, and Boyce's firm thrived.

GROWTH FOR THE CLIENT'S BENEFIT

As the city of Sioux Falls has grown, the firm bearing Boyce's name has expanded in personnel and legal expertise

to serve the ever-changing needs of its clients, large and small.

In addition to representing many successful business and professional clients, the firm represents the two largest employers in South Dakota. Consequently, it has developed significant expertise and experience in the field of labor law, including worker's compensation and employee relations matters from the administrative level to the courts and even the legislature. The firm counsels employers in all areas, including real property, sales and income tax matters, and discrimination law.

Boyce, Murphy, McDowell & Greenfield has assisted its clients in

▲ GENE'S STUDIO

Since 1878, Boyce, Murphy, McDowell & Greenfield has brought together the finest in legal expertise for clients in Sioux Falls and beyond.

financing transactions for construction and expansion. In the municipal and industrial bond area, it has represented every facet of the industry, from borrow-

ers to lenders to underwriters, including cities, counties, and the State of South Dakota.

The firm serves its clients in traditional areas such as estate, gift, and charitable tax planning, as well as contemporary legal areas of environmental, computer, telecommunications, and disability law. Members of the firm are frequent lecturers to legal and other groups throughout the city and state on all of these areas of law.

Boyce, Murphy, McDowell & Greenfield is intensively involved in the ever-expanding health care area and provides legal services to one of the city's major hospitals, its largest clinic, physicians' groups, nursing homes, and other health care providers of all sizes. The firm has also developed an expertise in the financing and licensing of health care facilities.

Actively involved in trial work before courts and administrative agencies, Boyce, Murphy, McDowell & Greenfield represents those injured in accidents, as well as claimants in construction, business, and commercial matters. Whether hired by the defendant or by an insurance company, the firm also represents those against whom claims are made. Its litigators have been hired as special counsel to the State of South Dakota and several of its government boards and agencies.

"We are large enough to have expertise in most areas our clients encounter, yet small enough that each client's problem receives individual attention," says Jeremiah D. Murphy, a partner in the firm.

DIVERSE LEGAL EXPERTISE

Boyce, Murphy, McDowell & Greenfield, headquartered since 1975 in the Norwest Bank Center in downtown Sioux Falls, has 10 partners today. Murphy represents corporate clients such as John Morrell & Co. and Citibank, which keeps him involved in governmental relations and lobbying. He also practices in the area of estate planning. Russell R. Greenfield, longtime legal adviser to the Sioux Falls Development Foundation, devotes his practice to the areas of municipal bonds, corporation law, and estate planning. David J. Vickers practices primar-

Left: Thomas J. Welk, Gregg S. Greenfield, Michael S. McKnight, and Terry N. Prendergast. Above: Jeremiah D. Murphy and James E. McMahon.

ily in the civil litigation, worker's compensation, and insurance defense areas. Gary J. Pashby, former president of the State Bar of South Dakota, engages in civil litigation, products liability, and insurance defense.

Vance R.C. Goldammer, former managing editor of the *South Dakota Law Review*, emphasizes creditors rights, corporation law, and banking law. Thomas J. Welk, a former Assistant and Deputy Attorney General of South Dakota, concentrates his practice in the areas of administrative, civil litigation, and health care law.

Terry N. Prendergast devotes his practice to commercial, corporation, and banking law and does civil litigation. James E. McMahon, a former Assistant Attorney General of South Dakota, is a trial lawyer.

Douglas J. Hajek's principal areas of practice include banking, municipal finance, corporation, and real estate law. Michael S. McKnight practices in the areas of worker's compensation and civil litigation.

Gregg S. Greenfield is an associate of the firm, emphasizing civil litigation and environmental law. John McDowell, who joined the firm in 1936, serves "of counsel" to the firm. Nine other employees, including secretaries and paralegal and accounting professionals, complete the staff.

"We believe that our wide range of legal professionals helps us to serve an equally wide range of clients," says Murphy. "This firm is dedicated to Sioux Falls and its citizens. Our tradition of service and community spirit has continued unabated since the firm's founding in 1878."

A LEADING LAW FIRM

Boyce, Murphy, McDowell & Greenfield has long been considered one of the community's leading legal firms. Representative local clients include John Morrell & Co., McKennan Hospital, SoDak Distributing, Central Plains Clinic, US West Communications, Sioux Falls Development Foundation, and the Catholic Diocese of Sioux Falls. Among the national clients the firm has served are the Ford Motor Co., Sears Roebuck & Co., First National Bank of Chicago, and General Electric Company. The firm also serves as counsel to a number of area banks, including Norwest Bank, Western Bank, Citibank (South Dakota), N.A., and The First National Bank in Sioux Falls.

Highly regarded for its expertise in insurance matters, the firm currently handles litigation for The St. Paul Companies, The Hartford Insurance Cos., American States Insurance, Aetna Life and Casualty, American Family Insurance, Design Professionals Insur-

ance Company, Prudential Insurance Co., The Equitable Life Assurance Society, and United Fire and Casualty Co., among other insurance industry leaders.

The members of the firm recognize important obligations to the community and state. In fulfilling these responsibilities, they have served as board members and volunteers for the Sioux Falls Area Chamber of Commerce, Development Foundation, Forward Sioux Falls, United Way, other civic and service organizations, and charitable, educational, religious, and health care agencies. Taking a leadership role in moving Sioux Falls forward has been as much a part of the firm's long history as its position of eminence in the legal community.

In addition to legal expertise and dedication to the welfare of Sioux Falls, the firm's longtime stability has been crucial to its success and longevity. "During all the critical periods of this community's development," says Russell Greenfield, "there has always been a Boyce law firm—for three generations in the Boyce-Greeley Building and for nearly a generation in our current offices. The firm is pleased that it has been a part of the growth of the city of Sioux Falls and looks forward to the continuing challenge of the future."

SIOUX FALLS COLLEGE IS A CHRISTIAN LIBERAL ARTS institution affiliated with the American Baptist Churches in the U.S.A., but has welcomed students of every faith and denomination for 120 years. ◆ Accredited by the North Central Association of Colleges and Schools, Sioux Falls College today has an enrollment of nearly 1,000. A wide range of financial aid is available to students, including scholarships, grants, college work study, and off-campus employment.

Spiritual life at Sioux Falls College is a unique quality of the campus experience. While all students are challenged to consider the importance of spiritual life, campus ministry recognizes the diversity of the student body. As a result, participation is a matter of personal choice. A variety of organizations and special interest clubs exist to help each student become actively involved in campus life.

Built in 1908, Jorden Hall is a historic landmark in Sioux Falls.

Music is an important element of the academic atmosphere at Sioux Falls College. The modern Jeschke Fine Arts Center, one of the region's premier performance venues, also houses the William Lee Bright Hall of Music. The Sioux Falls College Concert Chorale is acclaimed for its outstanding performances of sacred and secular choral music. The Singing Camerata, a select ensemble drawn from members of the Concert Chorale, performs in 16th century costume at the college's annual Madrigal Dinners. Chapel Choir, Symphonic Band, and Cougar Jam Jazz Ensemble all provide opportunities for student musicians to develop and exhibit their talents. In addition, the Dakota Wind Quintet, a professional ensemble of the South Dakota Symphony, is in residence at Sioux Falls College and is available for adjunct instruction.

The SFC theatre department produces several plays each year on the Meredith Auditorium mainstage and in the Arena Theatre in the Jeschke Fine Arts Center. Every other January, the music and theatre departments combine to produce a major musical. Most summers, the Coo Revue tours with a fast-paced theatrical revue show, performing for church camps, churches, and civic groups throughout the United States.

Sports at Sioux Falls College keep spectators on their feet. Competing in the South Dakota Intercollegiate Conference and National Association of Intercollegiate Athletics, SFC teams are consistently top competitors in a wide range of sports. Men's and women's teams compete in basketball, track, cross country, and tennis. Men's football and women's volleyball teams round out the intercollegiate offerings. The Stewart Wellness Center, a modern, state-of-the-art facility for sports training, provides a setting for varsity and intramural athletic competition among students.

Expanding its campus boundaries, Sioux Falls College has established cooperative relationships with Augustana College, the North American Baptist Seminary, USD, SDSU, and other colleges in Sioux Falls. The Kansai University of Foreign Studies in Osaka, Japan also provides special joint programs. Other unique opportunities include the Christian College Coalition's American Studies Program in Washington, D.C. and the Latin American Studies Program, which offers students an opportunity to live, work, and study in the heart of Latin America.

A SPIRIT OF SHARING

"We are enriched by all the diversity that God has created in the world," says Tom Johnson, president of the college. "Our campus brings together students from around the world, as well as older, non-traditional students and many business people from the community, in a spirit of sharing."

That spirit of sharing is the basis for two community outreach facilities on the Sioux Falls College campus. The Center for Management offers Certificate of Management and Management Excellence programs for professional growth. The unique programs include management courses and supervisory/ management development seminars led by national consultants.

Begun in 1976 as a service to the community, the on-campus Center for Women has grown into a comprehensive program touching the lives of over 2,000 women each year. The Center fulfills its commitment to helping women in personal, educational, and career development through programs which include career counseling, educational advising, personal counseling, development seminars, and networking with other women's groups. The Center for Women also serves as a resource and referral point for other community services.

In addition, the college's Twilight and Degree Completion programs allow non-traditional students and members of the community to continue their education at their own pace while pursuing a full-time career.

In an increasingly complex age, Sioux Falls College works for the development of intellectual excellence, emotional maturity, physical well-being, interpersonal skills, and personal values which reflect the character and teachings of Christ.

THE OLDEST BANK IN SIOUX FALLS OWES ITS LONGEVITY to a combination of service, stability, innovation, and family involvement, says William S. Baker, chairman of The First National Bank in Sioux Falls. ♦ One of just two local banks to survive the banking crisis of the late 1920s, First National Bank was founded in 1885 by a group of Sioux Falls citizens, several of whom are prominent figures in

state and local history. Organizing the capital and serving as the bank's first president was A.E. Sherman, father of the city's park system and donator of Sherman Park. Sherman assembled the first board of directors of what was then called the Minnehaha National Bank. One of the early directors was R.F. Pettigrew, a local businessman and South Dakota's first U.S. senator.

> "We keep an eye on technology, watching the advances being made in the industry," says William S. Baker, chairman. "But what is more important is that we lead in service. To do that, we need the combination of good people and technology that works."

Minnehaha National Bank grew by acquisition in its early days. In 1888, the bank merged with one-year-old Citizens National Bank. Sherman eventually stepped down as president to start the Union Trust Co., which merged with Minnehaha National in 1893.

BAKER AND KUEHN FAMILIES JOIN FORCES

It was shortly after the bank's founding that the Baker family became involved with Minnehaha National. William Lafayette Baker—grandfather of the bank's current chairman, William S. Baker, and its president, Robert S. Baker—migrated from upstate New York to begin his banking career in 1886. He became a cashier at Minnehaha National in 1889. Twenty-one years later, he was named president, the position he held until his death in 1939. During his 50 years with the

bank, Baker slowly acquired ownership. Today, the Baker family, and the family of Andrew Kuehn, an early investor in the bank and other Sioux Falls businesses, still control the bank.

William L. Baker guided the bank through the financially tumultuous 1920s and '30s. According to local banking history, the years following World War I brought a flurry of speculative activity. Land values soared, and second and third mortgages were common. Banking practices lacked the safeguards of today, and loans were easy to obtain. Then in 1924, as farm prices began to tumble and borrowers couldn't pay back their loans, local banks found themselves unable to meet the payment demands of their depositors. Within a year, most of the banks in Sioux Falls had failed. When the panic finally subsided, Minnehaha National was one of only two surviving banks.

According to family history, what kept the institution afloat during those tough times was the unwavering determination of the Bakers and the Kuehns to keep the doors open. "The two families had a lot of pride in the bank," says Curtis Kuehn, former president of the bank and grandson of Andrew Kuehn. "They went to bat for it during those times and provided capital to keep it going." Kuehn adds that Minnehaha National may have been more conservative than its competitors, thus avoiding some of the pitfalls of banking during that era.

In 1929, in a show of strength and optimism, the bank moved to impressive new quarters at 112 S. Phillips Avenue and changed its name to The First National Bank and Trust Company. The wooden building, which had formerly housed a furniture store, was extensively remodeled inside. On the front, a massive three-story sandstone

facade was erected, topped by the First National limestone eagle, which over the years has become a downtown Sioux Falls landmark. "It was a wooden structure with a beautiful stone front," remembers Chairman William S. Baker. "It looked substantial, but it wasn't."

That building was the bank's home until 1976, when the current facility was constructed at the corner of Phillips Avenue and Ninth Street in the very heart of Sioux Falls.

Since William L. Baker's death in 1939, the bank, which took its current name in 1952, has been guided by members of the Baker and Kuehn families. W.L. Baker was succeeded as president by Martin Kuehn, son of Andrew Kuehn, who held that post for three years. William Wiswall Baker, the son of William L. Baker, served as the bank's president from 1942 to 1971; he was followed by his son, William S. Baker, who remained president until 1983, when he became the bank's chairman, a position he currently holds. Curtis Kuehn guided the bank as president from 1983 until his retirement at the end of 1991. At that time, Kuehn was succeeded as president by Robert S. Baker, the current chairman's brother.

This three-story sandstone building, adorned by the First National Bank limestone eagle, was home to the bank for 47 years.

A fourth generation of Bakers and Kuehns is working in the bank today. William Ludlow Baker, son of chairman Baker, is a vice president, and Andrea Kuehn, daughter of Curtis Kuehn, is a trust officer and an assistant vice president. According to Chairman Baker, other children of the two families will have opportunities to join the bank if they choose. "We hope the next generation takes an interest in First National Bank as their forefathers have," he says.

BOOM TIMES AND CONTINUED GROWTH

First National Bank began a decade of rapid growth in the late 1960s that spread its presence geographically. The bank opened its first branch near the Western Mall in 1968. The Industrial Branch at 1600 West Russell Street followed in 1973, and a branch in the Empire Mall was added in 1975. The move to the new headquarters facility was made the following year.

Branches in the communities surrounding Sioux Falls were added soon after, with the acquisition of Dakota State Bank in Baltic and Dell Rapids in 1979 and their conversion into branches. More recently, branch banks have been acquired in Brandon and Valley Springs.

During the 1970s, First National installed Sioux Falls' first automated teller machines and established a regional teller machine network, the Advantage system. Today, the Advantage ATM network comprises over 50 percent of all ATM's in South Dakota. As a member of the CIRRUS system, First National makes Advantage banking possible in every state and in many cities around the world.

AN INDEPENDENT, LOCALLY OWNED BANK

With total assets of over $335 million and $289 million in deposits, First National Bank is today the largest independent locally-owned bank in the state. Chairman Baker attributes First National's strength and growth to many factors, including its independence and consistency of direction. "One of the true advantages of being independent," he says, "is that the people who make decisions are right here where customers are doing their banking."

And because of the two families' continued leadership of the bank, he says, the people who make the decisions today are going to be around tomorrow. At First National, longevity of officers and staff is a matter of pride. "Many people have spent their entire careers here," he adds.

Expanding Horizons, **a 12′ x 65′ copper relief sculpture created by Minneapolis artist William Saltzman, overlooks First National Bank's lobby at its main office.**

Other factors contributing to the bank's success, according to Baker, are the conservative banking philosophy handed down from the founders, an emphasis on customer service, and the diversity and innovation of its banking products. A state-of-the-art banking institution, First National strives to stay abreast of industry advances, incorporating them into its array of services to make banking more convenient for its customers.

"We keep an eye on technology, watching the advances being made in the industry," Baker says. "But what is more important is that we lead in service. To do that, we need the combination of good people and technology that works."

With service still the key today, just as it was in 1885, the Baker and Kuehn families continue the tradition of local banking that has made First National one of the most respected financial institutions in the region. From pioneer times to today—through economic depressions and recessions and the rapid industry changes of recent decades—the bank has enjoyed over a century of uninterrupted growth. The lessons learned and the standards set over the years promise to keep First National Bank strong through its second century of service.

Today, the limestone eagle, symboliz-
ing strength and stability, rests in front
of First National's main office at 9th
Street and Phillips Avenue.

WOODS, FULLER, SHULTZ & SMITH P.C. IS ONE of South Dakota's oldest and largest law firms with origins dating back more than 100 years. In 1887, a young attorney named Charles Olin (C.O.) Bailey arrived from Chicago on one of the five railroads that steamed into Sioux Falls, and established a local private law practice, laying the groundwork for the firm which more

than a century later is Woods, Fuller, Shultz & Smith.

During the 1940s and 1950s, the firm prospered on a staple of railroad and automobile litigation, complemented by a real estate and probate practice. M.T. Woods, H.L. Fuller, J.B. Shultz, and F.M. Smith, for whom the present-day firm is named, established a tradition of determination and hard work which serves as an example to those who have followed. As the field of law became more complex, Woods,

From left: **Richard O. Gregerson, Merle A. Johnson, and Arlo D. Sommervold are members of the firm's diverse legal team.**

Fuller, Shultz & Smith expanded, and its team of lawyers became increasingly specialized. Today, the firm is made up of legal professionals of diverse talents and interests, all of whom are committed to the same high standards that have earned the firm its reputation for excellence.

A DIVERSE TEAM

Traditionally, firm members have been active in state government, either in a legislative capacity or as lobbyists. Richard Gregerson was a state senator in the late 1970s and early 1980s and presently represents numerous organizations and companies as a lobbyist. A former FBI agent and Marine, Dick is active in politics and church affairs. William J. Janklow, former two-term governor for the state of South Dakota and Attorney General of South Dakota, is associated with the firm on an "of counsel" basis. Bill has lectured at Harvard Law School, Stanford Law School, UCLA Law School, and Rutgers, among other institutions of higher learning.

In the field of business law, the firm is involved in all aspects of corporate, commercial, employment, and real estate law. The business section of the firm is spearheaded by Merle Johnson, whose practice encompasses corporate and business law, as well as tax and estate planning. Merle is active in many

community activities and has made significant contributions to the Christian Legal Society and Christian Counseling Services. His amiable nature and sense of humor serve him well in the hectic and demanding field of business law.

Environmental law presents controversial issues to South Dakota businesses and citizens alike. William Taylor is on the cutting edge of environmental law, having previously served as a member of the South Dakota Board of Minerals and Environment (the state's environmental regulatory agency), and presently represents nu-

> Members of the firm are hard at work in virtually every area of the community, from church boards to boards of charitable organizations and from the Boy Scouts to Howard Wood Dakota Relays.

merous clients on environmental issues. He has participated in significant environmental policy decisions which have affected the state. His avid interest in the environment extends to his recreation time. Bill is an avid skier and has been known to do some rock climbing.

The firm's tax practice is led by Brad Grossenburg, who received a law degree from Hamline University in St. Paul, Minnesota and a Master of Law degree in taxation from the University of Florida. Complementing Brad is Mike Billion, a CPA, as well as a lawyer, who joined the firm in 1990 after 11 years as a partner in an accounting firm. He is a weekly contributor to the "Money Talks" column in the *Sioux Falls Argus Leader*.

In the 1980s, bankruptcy law leaped to the forefront of the South Dakota judicial system in volume alone. Roger Damgaard served as a law clerk for the United States Bankruptcy Court, District of South Dakota, before joining the firm in 1984. He has quickly developed a reputation as one of South Dakota's premier bankruptcy attorneys. Roger and others in the firm devote considerable time to the thorny issues of creditor/debtor rights.

LAWRENCE & SCHILLER

The thrust of the litigation practice at Woods, Fuller, Shultz & Smith includes personal injury, products liability, worker's compensation, and professional liability. The practice has expanded into securities litigation, civil rights, trademark infringement, and antitrust. The litigation section is headed by Arlo Somervold, who has earned notable courtroom victories in the areas of product liability and securities fraud. His impressive litigation record is complemented by his sharp wit and charm. Francis Smith is the exemplar. His distinguished legal career serves as an inspiration and ideal.

The specialized area of worker's compensation has been a significant component of the firm's growth. Comet Haraldson has been instrumental in the evolution of worker's compensation law in South Dakota, and his appearances before the South Dakota Supreme Court on issues of worker's compensation have served as key precedents in this quickly changing area of the law. Comet's specialized practice contrasts with his varied interests. He toured with a rock and roll band prior to starting his legal career. His recreational pursuits of motorcycling, flying, and snow skiing always keep him on the move.

The firm's office is located on South First Avenue in Sioux Falls.

Woods, Fuller, Shultz & Smith prides itself on the quality of its support staff. Its secretaries and paralegals are career professionals who take pride in being familiar with the files they work on. They know the right questions to ask, and act as valuable assistants to the lawyers. Their knowledge and assistance help alleviate the frustration clients often feel when attempting to reach a lawyer who, due to a court

Barbara Anderson Lewis and J.G. Shultz confer in the firm's law library.

appearance or client conference, cannot immediately take a call. The training the members of the support staff have received allows them to serve as safety nets for busy lawyers, ensuring that deadlines are met, phone calls are returned, appointments are kept, and documents are completed when needed.

BEYOND THE COURTROOM

Participation in community organizations and activities is a high priority at Woods, Fuller, Shultz & Smith. Members of the firm are hard at work in virtually every area of the community, from church boards to boards of charitable organizations and from the Boy Scouts to Howard Wood Dakota Relays. Elks, Rotarians, Kiwanians, and Lions abound. It is a rare occasion when a group of Sioux Falls citizens gathers to address a community need and at least one member of the firm is not present.

Despite their unified dedication to the legal profession, once outside the office the firm's lawyers and support staff participate in as many diverse activities as there are members of the firm. Under the supposedly staid legal exterior, there are not only the traditional golfers, but motorcyclists, pilots, skiers, horseback riders, a hot air balloonist, a rollerblader, a karate enthusiast, bridge aficionados, a guitarist in a rock band, skeet shooters, tennis champions, and a violinist, to name a few.

The legal expertise, professional pride, community service, and zest for outside interests at Woods, Fuller, Shultz & Smith combine to persuade those who come in as clients to remain as friends.

Woods, Fuller, Shultz & Smith thrives on the team concept. The individuals mentioned are just a few members of the team. The attorneys and support staff share their expertise, talents, and experience for the best interest of the client. Collectively and individually, the members of Woods, Fuller, Shultz & Smith strive to provide their clients with prompt, responsive, quality legal work. All recognize that the firm exists for the sole purpose of serving its clients.

SINCE ITS BEGINNING NEARLY A CENTURY AGO, Sioux Valley Hospital has cared for over 1 million patients. Along the way, the hospital has helped make Sioux Falls a major regional medical center, providing medical services that once were not possible in a city its size. ♦ Most of all, Sioux Valley is a community hospital, living daily a hospital-wide commitment to keeping costs low and the

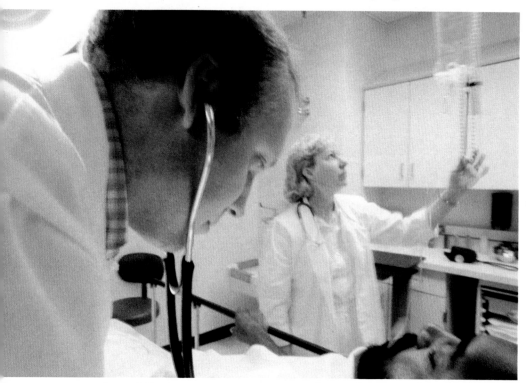

Sioux Valley's constant pursuit of perfection is mirrored daily in the professionalism of the medical staff and hospital personnel.

quality of medical care high. "You could say we believe in the old-fashioned concept of value," says Lyle Schroeder, Sioux Valley's president. "Over 100,000 patients a year use our inpatient and outpatient services. We have a commitment to them to offer high quality, technologically advanced medical care at affordable rates."

Sioux Valley's definition of community doesn't stop at the city limits. Its expanding campus does much more than serve local residents and those who travel to Sioux Falls for care. It also

houses the Sioux Valley Office of Rural Health, which offers assistance to communities in South Dakota, southwest Minnesota, and northwest Iowa through a variety of personnel and programs designed to enhance services already available.

Likewise, Sioux Valley brings expertise in sound medical center management to a group of hospitals throughout the tri-state area. While the individual hospitals maintain autonomy, Sioux Valley's personnel and technological resources are available to upgrade existing local services. Physicians, staff, and board members of rural hospitals can turn to Sioux Valley for additional training, and staff members often travel from Sioux Falls to the rural hospitals to help solve specific problems.

SETTING STANDARDS OF EXCELLENCE

Achieving excellence is a way of life at Sioux Valley Hospital. That constant pursuit of perfection is mirrored daily in the professionalism of the medical staff and hospital personnel. Committed to maintaining the finest equipment and facilities, Sioux Valley offers a variety of services that local residents have come to rely upon.

For example, Sioux Valley Hospital took a leadership role in providing much-needed cardiac services in the mid-1960s. The first patient was seen at the Sioux Valley Cardiac Catheterization Laboratory in 1978, and the first bypass surgery was performed a week later. Today, four "cath" labs serve the region. Nearly 50 percent of the lab's patients need bypass surgery, which translates into more than 10 open heart surgeries each week. Advanced treatment techniques like coronary balloon angioplasty and the administration of streptokinase and TPA are being used on a regular basis, along with electrophysiology and cardiac ablation.

An important new addition to the Sioux Valley Hospital campus is the Heart Center. Attached to the hospital's main building, the Heart Center offers the highest level of cardiac services in the area. Adjacent to the Cardiac Catheterization Laboratory, the center's four floors include three dedicated cardiac operating rooms, a surgical intensive care unit, a cardiac rehabilitation area, and a coronary intensive care unit. The cardiac specialists at the Sioux Valley Heart Center are top professionals, recognized as leaders in their field.

Sioux Valley Hospital's broad commitment to excellence in health care encompasses a dedication to medical education, research, and the promotion of wellness in Sioux Falls and communities throughout the four-state region.

Neonatal care is another area of expertise at Sioux Valley Hospital. In 1977, South Dakota had the lowest neonatal survival rate in the nation. The following year, the Sioux Valley Intensive Care Nursery/High Risk Obstetrics Program was upgraded and has since given thousands of newborns a second chance at life. The visionary facility also provides care for high risk mothers—women with diabetes, heart disease, hypertension, and other sensitive conditions. The Intensive Care Nursery is just one facet of Sioux Valley's Family Centered Maternity Care, which is designed to allow the entire family to share in the miracle of birth.

Since it introduced the concept of same day surgery to the local community in 1978, Sioux Valley Hospital has been a pioneer in the field. Initiated as a way to apply advances in medical technology and care to reduce the length of hospital stays for common surgical procedures, the Same Day Surgery Center operates as a separate facility within the hospital. The center has its own operating rooms, specially designed patient areas, and a full-time staff experienced in all facets of outpatient care. Today, over 100 different procedures can be performed at the Same Day Surgery Center. Each year, its staff performs several thousand individual procedures, giving patients even greater value without sacrificing medical excellence.

While Sioux Valley's primary mission is caring for the sick and injured, the hospital also plays a leading role in the growing area of preventive medicine. In operation since 1989, the Sioux Valley Wellness Center is one of the region's foremost fitness and wellness facilities. The state-of-the-art center, located on West 49th Street in the rapidly growing southwestern corner of the city, offers its members a cushioned running or walking track with electronic pacing system, Cybex Eagle® weight training machines, a complete free weight center, and aerobic equipment including treadmills, stairclimbers, rowing machines, exercise bikes, and ski

machines. The Wellness Center also houses a 25-yard swimming pool and a private 4,000-square-foot aerobic room with a Bio-cushion® floor. Two sets of fully appointed locker rooms provide members with individual showers and lockers with keys, towels, and toiletries. In 1991, Sioux Valley added a physical therapy and rehabilitation program housed in a newly constructed addition to the Wellness Center.

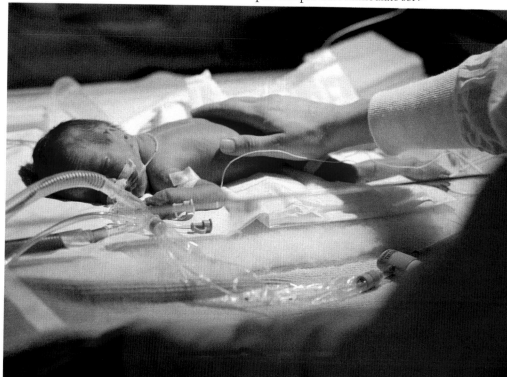

Since its upgrade in 1977, Sioux Valley's Intensive Care Nursery/High Risk Obstetrics Program has given thousands of newborns a second chance at life.

A LIFELINE TO THE REGION
Emergency care is yet another field in which Sioux Valley Hospital is a regional leader. With one of the most comprehensive trauma centers in the area, the hospital is equipped to handle everything from sprained ankles to heart attacks and serious injuries.

Sioux Valley's lifeline to the region is the Intensive Air transport system, which has provided ground and air transportation for critically ill, injured, and high-risk patients since it began service in 1977. Working in cooperation

with local physicians and emergency response teams, Intensive Air transports heart patients, accident victims, high risk expectant mothers, and sick infants to the hospital from their homes or the scene of an accident.

Sioux Valley's air transport fleet includes two fixed-wing air ambulance aircraft (both Beechcraft King Airs), as well as TRAUMA I, a twin-engine helicopter that provides immediate service throughout the four-state area of Nebraska, South Dakota, Iowa, and Minnesota. Specialty medical teams and the highest quality medical technology accompany the aircraft on emergency flights. The hospital also works with local emergency medical technicians to provide training and support in transporting patients to and from the hospital by ground ambulance.

BUILDING FOR TOMORROW
The constant growth of Sioux Valley Hospital's campus—located in the heart of Sioux Falls between 18th and 20th streets and Grange and Lake avenues—has been essential to allow the addition of new services and staff at the hospital. The recent decision to proceed with the planned South Expan-

For nearly 100 years, Sioux Valley Hospital has been growing to meet the ever-changing health care needs of the community. Today, this modern medical complex is undergoing an ambitious expansion project that will take it into its second century of service.

sion was encouraged by an anticipated need in Sioux Falls and the region for expanded health care over the long term.

Included in the expansion project will be a freestanding Outpatient Surgery Center, adjacent to a new parking ramp with space for 1,000 automobiles. Over a three-year period from 1989 to 1991, outpatient services grew 41 percent, making the need for expanded outpatient surgery apparent. This user-friendly center will be reached from the

new South Commons, continuing the Sioux Valley commitment to medical excellence and value.

Another part of the major expansion effort, the South Patient Building will house the Sioux Valley Hospital Women's and Children's Services, Radiation Oncology, Endoscopy, and additional outpatient services. With Sioux Valley already playing a major role in women's health issues through the establishment of the Breast Health Institute and the non-surgical Mammotest, the Women's and Children's Services addition is a critical component of the hospital's future goals in serving the community.

"You could say we believe in the old-fashioned concept of value," says Lyle Schroeder, Sioux Valley's president. "Over 100,000 patients a year use our inpatient and outpatient services. We have a commitment to them to offer high quality, technologically advanced medical care at affordable rates."

A fifth and sixth level are being added to Sioux Valley's existing patient care tower, providing 88 additional private patient rooms. Construction on the new floors was begun in the summer of 1992.

The construction of a power plant to heat, cool, and provide emergency power to the new buildings, and the addition of streets, lighting, and landscaping to the expanded campus are also planned. Space is provided in the master plan for the construction of a 50- plus unit hotel/motel with adjacent parking and an all-weather connection to the hospital for families of patients or out-of-town patients who are taking advantage of outpatient services.

As a teaching hospital, Sioux Valley is continuing a long history of commitment to improving health care through education. Since the hospital's founding, thousands of nurses from statewide programs and medical residents in family practice and other specialties have completed their education at Sioux Valley. The School of Nursing at Sioux Valley graduated thousands of nurses from 1894 until 1986. Today, the School of Radiologic Technology and the Medical Technologist School prepare students for carers in medical technology. Ground was also broken in the summer of 1992 for the University of South Dakota Health Sciences Center on the Sioux Valley campus. This 80,000-square-foot facility will house academic offices, classrooms, laboratories, and clinical space.

A REPUTATION FOR EXCELLENCE

Sioux Valley Hospital's broad commitment to excellence in health care encompasses a dedication to medical education, research, and the promotion of wellness in Sioux Falls and communities throughout the four-state region. As it looks to the future, the hospital endeavors to stay on the cutting edge of programs, research projects, and treatment methods.

Sioux Valley was recognized for its efforts when *Modern Healthcare* magazine named it one of the nation's "Top 100 Hospitals." In a ranking of hospitals that provide Medicare services, Sioux Valley was distinguished as one of 59 facilities with a significantly lower than expected death rate for Medicare patients, and one of just 16 hospitals in the United States to make that list for three consecutive years. In addition, *Coping* magazine named Sioux Valley Hospital one of the top 100 comprehensive cancer centers in the country. *Money* magazine, in naming Sioux Falls America's best place to live in 1992, cited the community's health care quality and referred specifically to Sioux Valley's tradition of excellence.

But hospital officials believe the best possible care extends beyond the most modern treatments and techniques. Excellence requires a unique, personal touch. To that end, a dedicated team of doctors, nurses, therapists, technicians, and support staff, as well as an active volunteer board, constantly strive to help patients and their families understand and cope with all phases of illness and recovery.

For nearly a century, that has been the Sioux Valley Hospital commitment: medical staff and medical science working together to bring leadership, excellence, and value to patients and families throughout the region.

Attached to the hospital's main building, the Sioux Valley Heart Center offers the highest level of cardiac services in the area.

Y THE TURN OF THE CENTURY IN SIOUX FALLS, several meat processing and packing companies had come and gone, unable to sustain successful operations. Then in 1909, John Morrell & Co. of England leased a downtown Sioux Falls building, which had previously been used as a meat-packing plant, and set about defying predictions of failure and making its third location in the United

States an unqualified success. Today, the Sioux Falls operation of John Morrell is one of the largest meat processing plants in the United States, and the largest plant that processes two major livestock species—hogs and sheep—at a single location. It is also the flagship plant for the company, which today is owned by Chiquita Brands International of Cincinnati, Ohio. John Morrell still operates from its original location at the foot of Weber Avenue, but over time has added 113 buildings on 88 acres to accommodate company growth.

Plant statistics reflect the sheer size and the remarkable production efficiency of the Sioux Falls operation. Each day John Morrell & Co. slaughters 15,000 hogs and 500 sheep. The carcasses are separated into cuts which are shipped directly to wholesale customers or routed to plant departments for processing into some 2,500 products, including smoked meats, bacon, canned meats, sausages, lard, and shortening.

About 350,000 pounds of pork and lamb are processed each hour, and approximately 16 million pounds of finished product are shipped from the plant every week. Non-edible, unfinished materials, such as hides, hair, casings, and glands, are sold to companies that produce leather, pharmaceuticals, and other goods.

John Morrell & Co. spends about $650 million yearly on the purchase of livestock, and its livestock slaughter would consume approximately one-fourth of South Dakota's annual corn crop.

BRITISH BEGINNINGS

The forerunner of John Morrell & Co. was established in 1827 by George Morrell, father of the company's namesake, in Bradford, England. Morrell got his start by buying a barge load of oranges and selling them for a profit on the streets of the city. After that original success, the family continued to buy and sell fruit, later expanding to vegetables and meat. In the mid-1850s, son John Morrell, who by that time was president of the company, moved the

headquarters to Liverpool, England and expanded the business to Ireland, Canada, and the United States.

"Our goal is to become not only the most progressive meat processing plant in the industry, but also the safest," says Tim Sinskey, plant manager.

In 1871, John Morrell & Co. opened its first U.S. meat-packing plant in Chicago. A second facility was opened in Ottumwa, Iowa, followed by the Sioux Falls plant in 1909. In the 1960s, Chiquita Brands International purchased John Morrell, which is the oldest meat-packing company in continuous operation in the United States. Of the original three U.S. facilities, only the Sioux Falls plant remains. Today, other John Morrell plants are located in Wilson, North Carolina and in Sioux City and Humboldt, Iowa.

Opposite and above: John Morrell & Co. employs more than 2,800 local residents at its 88-acre site in Sioux Falls.

The Sioux Falls meat processing facility, the largest industrial plant in the state, is a major force in the city's economy. Over 2,800 employees, representing a $68 million annual payroll, report each day to the plant. In 1991, the company's annual utility payment totaled $7 million, and its storage fee was $2.6 million. Other local companies also benefit from the plant's annual transportation expense, which in 1991 reached $14.3 million.

Also part of the Sioux Falls operation are 300 sales representatives, based throughout the country, who aid in the distribution of the plant's products to 8,000 customers in 46 states, as well as Japan, Korea, and Mexico.

QUALITY, INNOVATION, AND SAFETY

The 83-year-old Sioux Falls plant has a long-standing history of commitment to product quality, efficiency, and innovation in all aspects of its operations. In recent years, the plant has instituted "quality teams," composed of employees from all levels of the company, who discuss issues of common concern and develop programs to increase product or plant efficiency and quality. One of these teams, called "Waste Watchers," has helped develop recycling programs for aluminum cans, fiber vats, plastic barrels, white and computer paper, and scrap metals. Plans are also under way to extend the recycling program to even more of the plant's waste materials.

A major commitment of the facility's management team is to provide the safest work environment possible for its employees. To that end, a full-time industrial technician develops accident prevention programs and analyzes individual workstations to both improve efficiency and ensure safety. On staff at Morrell's new and enlarged medical facility are seven nurses and a full-time physician who treat employees for any type of medical problem, but also specialize in treating the muscle soreness and strain that can accompany a physically rigorous job. The medical staff and personnel department have instituted regular "stretch" breaks for all plant employees and twice-a-day exercise workouts for new employees to condition them for their jobs.

"Our goal is to become not only the most progressive meat processing plant in the industry, but also the safest," says Tim Sinskey, plant manager. "We're consistently making improvements in our operation, and we intend to be the nation's leader in setting new standards for the meat processing industry."

A LEADING CORPORATE CITIZEN

With more than eight decades of local history and the energy and commitment of both management and the plant work force, John Morrell & Co. has woven itself into the very fabric of the Sioux Falls community. As one of the city's most prominent corporate citizens, the company annually contributes monetary and product gifts to over 100 charities and civic groups, including the United Way, Children's Inn, Threshold, Turn About, American Cancer Society, American Lung Association, PTA groups, Chamber of Commerce, Youth Enrichment Services, Scouting, youth sports teams, Sioux Empire Arts Council, South Dakota Symphony, and the Entertainment League. The company also actively supports agricultural groups such as 4-H and Future Farmers of America, as well as many farmer appreciation events in the tri-state area.

With a longtime dedication to the community, its employees, and the quality of its products, John Morrell & Co. resolves to maintain its leading position in the country's meat processing industry and as a local corporate citizen.

MANY OF SIOUX FALLS' MOST NOTEWORTHY BUILD-ings have been erected by Sioux Falls Construction, the city's oldest construction firm. ◆ The Coliseum, home of symphony concerts and other special events, was built in 1917. Penmarch Place in south Sioux Falls was completed in 1927 for the Foster family, then owners of John Morrell & Co. Over the years, the company has also built

the Sioux Falls Community Playhouse (originally the Orpheum Theatre), the Minnehaha Country Club, the YMCA, and the historic Central Fire Station (1912).

The company was established in 1910 by three Sioux Falls businessmen: William Snitkey, Robert A. Perkins, and Charles S. Miller. Five years later Leonard F. Boyce, a native of Sioux Falls and a recent graduate of the University of Minnesota, returned to the city to join the company. It wasn't long before he had acquired the others' interest in the firm. His son, Frank L. Boyce, joined Sioux Falls Construction in 1950 and today serves as chairman of the board.

"We're a flexible construction company with many areas of expertise," says Frank Boyce. "We've built every kind and size of public and commercial structure, from hospitals to parking ramps, in our 80-plus years of service to the Sioux Falls area and the region."

Recent projects include the construction of the Encore Radisson Hotel in the southwest section of Sioux Falls, the addition to and remodeling of Home Federal Savings Bank, the remodeling of Westward Ho Country Club, and the construction of the Dakota Midwest Cancer Institute. In 1990, Sioux Falls Construction opened a new area to commercial development by completing the Bank of New York complex in southwest Sioux Falls.

HANDLING CHALLENGES FROM START TO FINISH

Sioux Falls Construction is known for its ability to handle major jobs from start to finish—a reputation that has led to some unique challenges. "We built a school on the Cheyenne River Indian Reservation, which is in the middle of the state near the Cheyenne River," Boyce says. "Upon completion, the

campus was virtually a city in itself. We constructed roads, the water tower, and a sewage treatment system, in addition to the classrooms, auditorium, and residences for the faculty, and we had to bring in electricity from 25 miles away."

The company also has years of experience in infrastructure construction. The original Sioux Falls sewage treatment plant, the first Sioux River spillway near the state penitentiary in Sioux Falls, and the 18th Street bridge near Southeastern Drive were all built by Sioux Falls Construction. One of the company's toughest infrastructure jobs, Boyce recalls, was a poured-concrete sanitary sewer in Papillion, Nebraska, which was one mile long, 12 feet deep, and 12 feet wide.

A major Sioux Falls Construction project now under way is the remodeling of the exterior of the US West Building in downtown Sioux Falls. This building serves as the home of the telephone company's regional offices. Boyce describes the project as similar to being on an archaeological dig: "The building has been added onto, remodeled, and refaced over the years, and in the course of completing the exterior work, we uncovered the original brick building. It's still a fine, strong structure. The new exterior is going to be a bold, new look for their offices, and we're excited to be a part of it."

TODAY AND TOMORROW

Sioux Falls Construction has kept pace with the city it calls home, growing steadily over the years. The firm now employs 150 people during the height of the construction season. These employees work on projects located throughout the region. Each project is supervised by a team of eight administrators and engineers who ensure quality control and construction excellence.

Sioux Falls Construction is well known for its work on local office towers and historic landmarks, but the company guarantees the same level of enthusiasm and quality for projects of all sizes. From bridges to schools and from churches to hotels, Sioux Falls Construction Company continues to be an important partner in the growth and development of Sioux Falls.

Sioux Falls Construction completed the Central Fire Station (top) in 1912. Today, the firm is adding a new exterior to the US West regional office (bottom).

Over the years, the firm has completed a variety of local projects: the Boyce-Greeley Building (top left), Lincoln Senior High School (bottom left), and the city sewage plant (above).

Top: More recently, Sioux Falls Construction completed a striking addition to the McKennan Hospital campus.

THE SIOUX FALLS OF 1907 WAS A BUSTLING PLACE. Population was over 10,000 and growing, businesses such as a foundry, brewery, and broom company were flourishing, and a modern electric trolley system replaced its horse-drawn predecessors. That same year, a group of Sioux Falls business people incorporated the Chamber of Commerce, with First National Bank president William L.

The Chamber is housed in the Commerce Center at 200 North Phillips Avenue.

Baker serving as the organization's first president.

From its inception, through *Money* magazine's naming of Sioux Falls as "America's Best Place to Live" in 1992, the Sioux Falls Area Chamber of Commerce has been instrumental in addressing the issues and controversies of the day. During its early years, the Chamber supported local citizens as they twice changed the form of city government, argued over the 10-mile-per-hour speed limit (which many considered reckless), allowed early automobiles, installed new sewer lines, and struggled with the community's extraordinary growth.

Although the Chamber maintains its proactive stance on current issues and events, in the past few decades the organization has broadened its role to include planning for the future, setting long-term goals, and implementing programs to encourage economic development. The Chamber's mission statement, refined and revised over the years, states: "As the leading Sioux Falls business advocate, we represent our members by advancing and promoting the economic health of the region."

AN ADVOCATE FOR SIOUX FALLS BUSINESS

One of the Chamber's first efforts in its expanded role was a program called ABCD, Attaining Balanced Community Development. Initiated in the late 1960s, the plan focused on the positive growth of the city. One of the business community's first successful volunteer programs, it was a joint effort of the Chamber and the Sioux Falls Development Foundation.

Outgrowths of ABCD, which was active through the early '70s, were the Holiday Inn City Centre, a much-needed facility for large conventions; the expansion of the airport into a

regional facility with national carriers; and the construction of the Sioux Falls Arena.

The 1970s saw the establishment of the Convention and Visitors Bureau, a division of the Chamber which plays a critical role in fulfilling its mission. The CVB works with the community's growing hospitality industry to bring revenue-producing conventions and large meetings to Sioux Falls, and to promote the city as a vacation stop for tourists in the region.

In the 1980s, when the business community feared Sioux Falls might soon face a stagnant period of economic growth, the Chamber teamed up, once again, with the Sioux Falls Development Foundation to create Forward Sioux Falls. Organized in 1987, this

From left: Joe P. Kirby, chairman-elect; Jim Schmidt, immediate past chairman; and Gary Olson, chairman.

comprehensive marketing program to promote economic development created strategies to encourage new job opportunities and increase capital investment in Sioux Falls.

Supported by $1.8 million in private funds donated by area businesses, the program succeeded beyond the dreams of its founders. More than 6,500 new jobs and over $300 million in capital investment resulted from the program. Forward Sioux Falls II, the program's second phase, has raised $2.1 million since its beginning in January 1992.

The Chamber's leadership and membership have also developed a 10-point action program to be implemented over a five-year period beginning in 1992. Elements of the program include identifying critical issues in the business environment, market positioning of the business community, promoting a strong educational system, providing new managers with needed information to facilitate their involvement in the community and the Chamber, and increasing member involvement through a committee structure based on the Chamber's mission and needs.

In addition, major divisions of the Chamber, including Agri-business, Public Affairs, and Membership, work to further economic development in the city and effectively represent the diverse interests and concerns of the business community.

Now in its 10th decade of service, the Sioux Falls Area Chamber of Commerce is an organized and effective body of volunteers united in their mission and goals. The success of the retail, medical, and service industries, combined with the quality of life in Sioux Falls which led *Money* magazine to rank the community first among 300 metropolitan areas, parallels the Chamber's commitment to business. An advocate for the Sioux Falls business community since 1907, the Chamber has a long history of success in promoting and advancing the economic health of the area.

FROM TEAMS OF HORSES HAULING COAL ACROSS TOWN to modern trucks carrying digitized computer images across the country, Parker Transfer & Storage has reflected the growth and progress of Sioux Falls for more than 80 years. Today's company, the largest commercial mover in the state, grew out of the merger of two transportation firms run by different branches of the same family. ◆ The roots

of the business were established in 1911 when William Munce purchased a Sioux Falls dray line for $100 and started Munce Bros. The company had over 20 head of top quality horses that hauled household items, coal, livestock, heavy machinery, and other goods for the growing community. In 1956, the management of the company was turned over to the next generation when William Munce handed the reins to his sons, Howard and Kenneth.

Meanwhile, Walter Parker, a former Munce Bros. employee, purchased his own dray line in 1926 with his wife, Mable Munce Parker, a sister of the Munce brothers. By 1935, Parker Transfer operated the largest commercial warehouse in the state and was one of the city's major household and commercial carriers.

UNITING TWO FAMILY FIRMS

On July 1, 1987 the two family businesses were brought together through a merger to form one larger, stronger company. Jeff Parker, grandson of the founder, today serves as president of the firm. Headquartered in the Airport Industrial Park, the company employs 18 people and maintains a fleet of 25 trucks.

Parker Transfer & Storage is known for some of the largest and most complicated moving jobs in Sioux Falls. In the summer of 1992 when Central Plains Clinic moved to a new facility, Parker Transfer & Storage carried all the records, equipment, and furnishings in a huge, four-day effort that utilized all the company's vehicles and personnel.

The company continues to expand its storage business, as well. A 16,000-square-foot warehouse at 221 South

Franklin, which Munce Bros. built in 1967, is today a state-of-the-art, climate-controlled document storage facility. The 100,000-square-foot warehouse at Parker's headquarters stores hardgoods of every description, from caskets and household appliances to portions of the U.S. honey crop.

Over the years, the firm has made the jump from horse-and-wagon hauling to sophisticated transfer and storage technology by providing outstanding service. With its strong foundation and record of success, Parker Transfer & Storage will continue to play a major role in the economic life of Sioux Falls.

In 1987, a merger brought together two venerable family businesses: Munce Bros., founded in 1911, and Parker Transfer, established in 1926. The larger, stronger company that resulted continues to build on the reputation for excellence that its predecessors have enjoyed for decades in Sioux Falls and beyond.

ARING IS A LONG-HELD TRADITION AT MCKENNAN Hospital in Sioux Falls. The 407-bed, general short-term acute care facility was established in 1911 by the Presentation Sisters of Aberdeen, South Dakota. Today, it is a member of the Presentation Health System, which includes 25 hospitals, clinics, and retirement homes across the Upper Midwest. ♦ Through the generosity of

Helen McKennan, a Sioux Falls native who provided start-up funds to create a new hospital, the original portion of today's 42-acre medical campus was constructed near the parcel of land she donated to the city for its first public park. Mrs. McKennan could not have foreseen the hospital's tremendous growth or the high-tech developments in health care that have come to Sioux Falls during the subsequent eight decades.

Over the years, the city's reputation as a regional medical center has been enhanced by developments at McKennan Hospital, including the recent opening of the Dakota Midwest Cancer

Institute and the relocation of Central Plains Clinic, the state's largest specialty and subspecialty clinic, to the McKennan campus.

With nearly 2,200 employees, today's McKennan Hospital is much like a small city unto itself. The campus has its own security services, well-lit parking ramps to accommodate up to 1,423 automobiles, and an all-weather skyway connecting the core group of buildings of this modern medical complex.

McKennan's staff of more than 300 physicians and dentists serve patients from South Dakota, northwestern Iowa, and southwestern Minnesota. Providing

a wide range of quality services, this tertiary care facility has also been a leader in bringing new services not found in other hospitals to the region. McKennan brought to Sioux Falls the only freestanding cancer institute, the only burn unit, the only inpatient rehabilitation therapy pools, the only hyperbaric oxygen unit, the only poison control center, and the only private psychiatric intensive care unit. The hospital was also the first to bring a CT scanner, a helicopter ambulance service, and an inpatient rehabilitation service to the region. McKennan's continuing commitment to progress is apparent in its plans to build a new women's and children's center to improve its obstetrical, pediatric, and women's health services.

LEADING THE FIGHT AGAINST CANCER

The McKennan Cancer Program is breaking new ground in the 1990s for cancer patients in the region. In the summer of 1989, the hospital began construction on the Dakota Midwest

Cancer Institute on the McKennan campus. The following year, the first phase of the project, the Radiation Therapy Center, was opened for use, complete with the campus' first state-of-the-art, high-energy linear accelerator for radiation therapy.

In the spring of 1991, the Dakota Midwest Cancer Institute was completed and now houses gynecological, pediatric, and medical oncology services, as well as neurosurgery treatment. Support services such as a patient education library, counseling center, and cancer registry are also available at the new center, which serves the five-state region of Minnesota, Iowa, Nebraska, and the Dakotas.

McKennan's inpatient Hospice Unit, in operation since 1986, underwent a major renovation and expansion in 1989. The Hospice Unit cares for cancer patients who are in the final stages of their illness and can no longer remain at home. Educational programs—such as the "Living with Cancer" series modeled after the American Cancer Society's "I Can Cope"

program, and special post-surgery, chemotherapy, and radiation therapy education—are another important part of the McKennan Cancer Program.

FAMILY CENTERED CHILDBIRTH

A unique commitment to family closeness and participation underlies every birth at the McKennan Hospital Childbirth Center. That unique philosophy of togetherness places great importance on making each new family feel at home; at McKennan, both mother and baby enjoy the highest level of care and safety without the cold, impersonal feel of a traditional operating room. In fact, the Childbirth Center has been carefully designed to be large enough to offer a wide range of birthing options, yet small enough to ensure a caring atmosphere for every mother and child.

The hospital also offers the comforting presence of a state-of-the-art Intensive Care Nursery, a facility staffed by experienced, professional neonatologists and neonatal nurse practitioners, all just steps away from McKennan's

LDR and LDRP rooms. These private, home-like suites for labor/delivery/recovery and labor/delivery/recovery/postpartum can be quickly converted to fully equipped delivery rooms. The comfortable suites are even designed to handle high-risk pregnancies. As a result, an expectant mother can remain in the same room throughout her stay at McKennan, reducing overall stress and helping her remain focused on the all-important task of delivering the new baby. In 1993, McKennan will open a new $13 million "hospital within a hospital" for women's and children's services.

AN EARLY DEDICATION TO MENTAL HEALTH

The first mental health care center in South Dakota was established at McKennan Hospital in 1958. The Behavioral Health Services Center, as the facility is known today, offers a holistic approach to psychiatric care, with a complete mental health program for patients of all ages. For example, the center's Acute Adult Program is a

Opposite: McKennan Hospital stands on a 42-acre campus in south central Sioux Falls.

Above: The region's only freestanding cancer institute, The Dakota Midwest Cancer Institute is located on the McKennan Hospital campus.

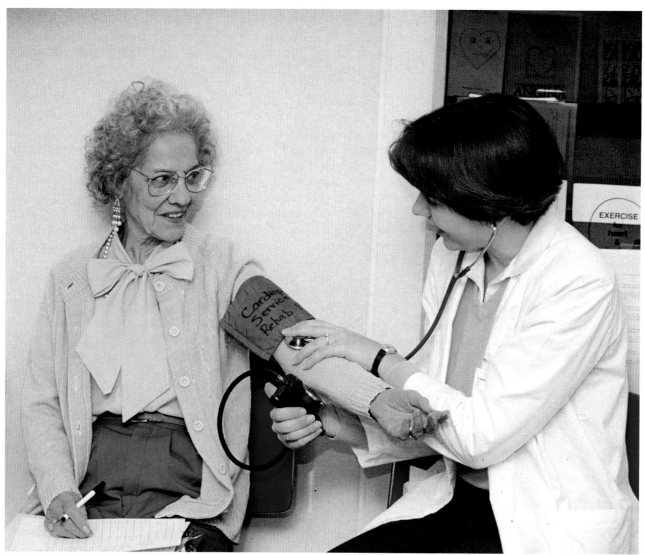

secure 14-bed inpatient unit dedicated to providing safe, compassionate care to adult mental health patients. Participants in the program benefit from a high staff to patient ratio which ensures close observation and much needed support.

The adult, senior, and adolescent programs provide specialized psychiatric care to people who require diagnostic evaluations for a wide range of cognitive, behavioral, and emotional dysfunctions. The center's entire staff is dedicated to short-term, specialized treatment aimed at returning these patients to their normal family, community, and work roles.

REHABILITATION SERVICES

Another innovative and highly successful program at McKennan is the Rehabilitation Center, a 44-bed comprehensive care facility located on the second floor of the hospital. Bright and contemporary in design, the unit is staffed by specially trained rehabilitation nurses. All patient rooms are private with careful attention given to the unique needs of rehabilitation patients.

A variety of treatment options are available for patients who suffer from stroke, spinal cord injury, head injury, amputations, chronic pain, and carpal tunnel syndrome. Perhaps the most unusual element of McKennan's rehabilitation program is Easy Street, a colorful, real-life setting in which patients work on mobility and daily living skills. The Easy Street environment includes a bank, grocery store, vending machines, greenhouse, and transitional living apartment, all designed to ease the patient's reentry into normal life.

Outpatients, including rehabilitation patients who have left the hospital, receive care at McKennan's Outpatient Rehabilitation Center at 50th and West-

McKennan Hospital's mission is to provide quality Christian care to all patients.

ern Avenue. As a critical component in each patient's full recovery, the center offers a range of outpatient services such as physical, occupational, and speech therapy.

EMERGENCY SERVICES

Another facet of McKennan's tradition of caring is the Emergency/Trauma Center. Specially trained nurses and doctors deliver expert care around the clock for trauma, spinal injuries, burns, behavioral problems, cardiac emergencies, and poisonings. Equipped to handle every type of emergency for patients of all ages, McKennan's Emergency/Trauma Center provides individualized treatment and special consideration for children and families. The center is also the focal point for all

Easy Street helps rehabilitation patients "relearn" everyday tasks.

specialized trauma services of the hospital, which in 1992 became the region's only health care facility verified as a trauma hospital by an inspection team from the American College of Surgeons.

Another important link in the emergency network for saving lives in Sioux Falls is the regional Poison Center at McKennan. Recognized by the American Association of Poison Control Centers as one of the best facilities of its kind in the nation, the center is manned by professional pharmacists who answer phone calls involving poison emergencies, and by doctors of clinical pharmacology and other emergency specialists who are available for consultation.

When every minute counts in an emergency situation, McKennan's Careflight is called into action. The first emergency helicopter transport service in South Dakota, Careflight was established in 1986 to speed the delivery of emergency care and to transport ill or injured adult and pediatric patients. The Bell Long Ranger II helicopter, with a 130 mph cruising speed and a two-patient capacity, reduces the time required for ground transport by up to 60 percent and can land in most flat areas, including parking lots, racetracks, and the roofs of reinforced buildings.

The Careflight team consists of pilots with over 2,500 hours of helicopter flight experience and registered nurses with a minimum of five years of critical care experience and certification in advanced cardiac life support and resuscitation. On the ground, emergency room doctors and trauma team members maintain constant communication with the airborne medical crew. Careflight's five-minute response time and 400-mile range, combined with its 24-hour, 365-day-a-year availability, make the service a powerful weapon in a life-threatening battle against time.

A COMMUNITY OF HEALTH CARE PROFESSIONALS

Since its founding in 1911, the hospital campus has grown to include a diverse and highly trained community of health care professionals. With the original hospital at its core, additional facilities and services have been added over the years to greatly extend McKennan's reach in Sioux Falls and beyond. The Sioux Falls Surgical Center (offering same-day surgical procedures), Central Plains Clinic, the McGreevy Clinic, Physicians Office Building, and the Dakota Midwest Cancer Institute all make the campus an indispensable regional health care resource.

Still today, McKennan's mission reflects the founding philosophy of the Presentation Sisters of Aberdeen: To provide the highest quality health care in an environment of Christian caring and respect for human dignity. This commitment, known throughout the region as "McKennan Cares," represents a sincere promise to each patient and family touched by McKennan Hospital.

Huge combines and four-wheel-drive tractors have modernized the harvest, but anyone who grew up in South Dakota in the 1930s and 1940s recognizes the processes involved in an old-time oats harvest.

Time was, the part of Sioux Falls near the 10th Street Viaduct was always smoky with the steam from rushing locomotives, like the one pictured here in 1950. Long after steam engines went the way of the horse and buggy, passenger trains continued to serve the city. The last one, the Milwaukee Road's Arrow, departed in 1965.

SPIRIT OF SIOUX FALLS 1914 - 1968

1914
Baumgartner's
Electric, Inc.

1919
Bell Paper Box, Inc.

1959
Culbert-Davis Co.

1915
Central Plains Clinic, Ltd.

1924
May, Johnson, Doyle
& Becker, P.C.

1960
McGladrey & Pullen

1916
Northern States
Power-South Dakota

1931
Sunshine Food Markets

1962
LCM/Nichols Institute

1917
Henry Carlson Company

1946
Egger Steel Company

1963
The Evangelical Lutheran
Good Samaritan Society

1917
Lakeside Dairy

1949
Midwest Coast Transport

1967
Fiegen Construction Co.

1918
Augustana College

1952
Sweetman Const. Co.

1968
Southeast Vocational
Technical Institute

WHEN TOM BAUMGARTNER WAS JUST A BOY, HE worked at his uncle's electrical shop pulling wire and conduit through small spaces where the grown men couldn't fit. At that age—and size—he did not know that he and his family would devote their lives to Baumgartner's Electric, Inc., a Sioux Falls success story with nearly 80 years' experience as an electrical subcontractor.

Baumgartner's Electric began in Sioux Falls when James Pryde, who learned his trade as an electrician in the coal mines of Pennsylvania, came west to South Dakota. In 1914, he and his wife Frances established an electrical contracting firm, Pryde Electric, in the young community of Sioux Falls. Mrs. Pryde's younger brother, Al Baumgartner, soon arrived in Sioux Falls where he worked briefly for his sister and brother-in-law before serving in World War I. After the war, he returned to Pryde Electric and in 1929, relocated to Rapid City to found Baumgartner's Electric Company.

When James and Frances Pryde decided to retire in 1952, Al Baumgartner's Rapid City firm acquired Pryde Electric. Tom Baumgartner, Al's son and a partner in the firm, returned to Sioux Falls to manage Pryde Electric under its new name, Baumgartner's Electric. In 1956, Tom bought out the other partners and acquired full ownership with his wife, Grace. Since his retirement in 1989, Tom has served the company in an advisory position.

In 1972, Tom's son Gary joined the firm as an apprentice electrician, representing the third generation of family involvement in the business. Over the years, he progressed to journeyman, master electrician, and estimator, gradually assuming a management role in the business.

A WHO'S WHO OF SIOUX FALLS LANDMARKS

Thanks to the longtime dedication of the Baumgartner family, the company has come far in Sioux Falls. Today, Baumgartner's Electric boasts 26 electricians and four clerical and administrative employees. The company's list of projects reads like a who's who of Sioux Falls landmarks. The new Washington High School and Roosevelt High School, four of the city's newest elementary schools, Southeast Vocational Technical Institute's campus, the IBM and Western Surety office buildings, Builders Square/Office Max, Alick's Valley Mall, and Radisson Encore Inn are just a few of the electrical design and construction jobs the firm has completed.

According to Gary Baumgartner, current president of the firm, many of the buildings are very familiar. "When we did the remodeling work on the old Lewis Southgate building, now Lewis Square," he says, "we replaced wiring the company had installed decades ago. In fact, one of my first jobs was to crawl above the plaster ceiling putting nuts on the light fixture hangers that the men held up from below. At that time, I was the only one small enough to get between the bar joists."

Often, it is new technology that brings the company back to a job Baumgartner's Electric originally wired. "Today's new equipment," says Gary Baumgartner, "from higher efficiency lighting to fiber optics and data transmission cabling for computer

▼ JOEL STRASSER

Baumgartner's Electric has completed many local electrical design and construction jobs, including Roosevelt High School (below) and the Western Surety building (above).

systems keeps us up to date. These innovations make it possible for us to improve electrical systems, saving the customer money along the way." For example, Baumgartner's Electric's recent relighting project for St. Joseph's Cathedral utilized specially designed lighting fixtures to make the building visible from throughout the city. At the same time, the more efficient fixtures cut power consumption by 70 percent allowing St. Joseph's Cathedral to qualify for a $1,000 rebate from Northern States Power Company.

For generations, Baumgartner's Electric has done electrical work for businesses throughout Sioux Falls. As today's employees return to update those buildings, they carry with them the commitment to quality craftsmanship and attention to detail that has characterized the firm since its founding in 1914.

"Our family has always believed in doing it right," Tom Baumgartner says. "I'm convinced that's one of the reasons we're still here today."

▲ JOEL STRASSER

BELL PAPER BOX, INC.

FOUNDED IN 1919, BELL PAPER BOX CO. FOR DECADES produced simple, usually unadorned, rigid boxes and lock-corner cartons for local bakeries and apparel and specialty stores. Today, the company manufactures approximately 4 million folding paper cartons each week in a variety of designs and colors for wholesale or retail customers across the country and the world. With paperboard it

"The bulk of our business is here in the United States, but we're reaching out," says Mark Graham, president. "Our goal is to give our customers outstanding service, no matter where they are."

purchases from several U.S. mills, Bell Paper Box, Inc. produces 15,000 tons of paper products annually.

A NEW DIRECTION

A new direction and growth surge at Bell Paper Box were initiated in 1976 when the company was purchased by Mark Graham, a former insurance salesman who learned of the company's availability through an ad in the *Argus Leader*. At that time the company employed only a handful of people and had annual sales of $40,000.

Quality control experts are consulted throughout the production process to get the best results every time.

"When I bought Bell Paper Box, I knew nothing about box manufacturing, production methods, printing, or any of the elements that go into making paper cartons," recalls Graham. "But I learned fast with the help of some key people I hired, and we approached our venture with a can-do attitude that still guides the company today."

One of Graham's first initiatives was to expand the company's marketing base by seeking out large wholesale distributors to sell its packaged products regionally and nationally. Bell Paper Box made further inroads into a larger, higher volume market in 1979 when the company introduced a new packaging product called Bone Guard. The advanced design of the product prevented the bone in a cut of meat from puncturing its plastic shipping

pouch, which had been a problem for meat packing companies. Bell Paper Box was soon supplying Bone Guard to major meat packers throughout the central United States, including John Morrell & Co., George A. Hormel, Armour Foods, Wilson Foods, Swift Independent, and Farmland Foods.

With subsequent improvements to the Bone Guard product, Bell Paper Box continued to build its reputation among meat packers. But a nationwide market foothold among other types of manufacturers was still out of the company's reach due to a lack of equipment.

In 1985, after careful research and study, Bell Paper Box took steps to increase its ability to compete effectively in a national arena: The company acquired a 60,000-square-foot building on West Algonquin Street to serve as a headquarters office and add more production space. It also purchased the equipment necessary to produce high quality, multi-color folding cartons in large quantities, investing over $1 million in two large printing presses—a five-color press and a six-color press— and high-speed die cutting machines. With these major improvements, a new era was ushered in at Bell Paper Box.

A LEADER IN QUALITY

While still a relative newcomer as a manufacturer of multi-color paper cartons, Bell Paper Box is acknowledged as an industry leader in quality and steadily attracts new customers. "The bulk of our business is here in the United States, but we're reaching out," says Graham. "We have shipped to Canada, Mexico, Spain, Belgium, and other parts of Europe. Our goal is to give our customers outstanding service, no matter where they are."

The company's reputation for quality and service is reflected in an annual growth rate of 30 percent in recent

years; sales for 1992 are projected at $20 million, a respectable share of the $5 billion folding paper carton industry. Today, Bell Paper Box employs 175 people and operates from three buildings encompassing 130,000 square feet—two production facilities and one warehouse all located in the Algonquin Street area.

From stocking paperboard rolls to caring for finished goods, Bell Paper Box provides excellent warehousing flexibility for its clients.

Graham attributes the company's amazing growth to excellent customer service, innovation, and the open-minded, affirmative attitude of its employees. "We're willing to try to do things others can't or won't," he says. "We'll consider a situation and ask 'Why not?' That has contributed greatly to our success."

NGUS ANSON DOESN'T HAVE A CRYSTAL BALL IN HIS office, but sometimes he wishes he did. The chief executive of Northern States Power-South Dakota (NSP-SD) spends a great deal of time thinking about providing excellent customer service to NSP customers. ♦ "With the growth Sioux Falls has experienced," Anson says, "it's important for us to listen, anticipate, and be responsive to our

NSP linemen Ken Berg and Joel Bialas place safety shields over electrical wires in preparation for some pole-top equipment installation.

customers' needs." That forward-looking philosophy, combined with a commitment to the environment, guides the day-to-day actions of NSP-SD. Northern States Power Company, founded in 1916 and based in Minneapolis, has been serving customers in the Sioux Falls area for over 75 years. But

rapid growth in Sioux Falls encouraged the company to establish NSP-SD as a separate business unit in January 1991. Today, NSP-SD serves 36 communities in southeastern South Dakota and 19 in southwestern Minnesota. The Sioux Falls base is also a dispatch headquarters, sending crews to assist 318,000 customers throughout the Northern States Power service area outside Minneapolis-St. Paul.

ENVIRONMENTAL CONCERN, ENERGY CONSERVATION

According to Anson, protecting the environment throughout the large NSP service area is a major concern of the company.

"Our commitment to the environment is part of our commitment to the community," he says. "NSP has instituted the BRITE program—Being Responsible In Today's Environment. We recycle everything, including paper and wood products, and we try to be a community leader in the recycling and energy conservation movement."

NSP realizes that an important aspect of any energy conservation plan is the conservation of electricity. Currently, NSP has several programs to help customers reduce the amount of electricity they use and save money on energy costs. For example, the company offers valuable rebates on lighting retrofits to encourage businesses to upgrade energy efficient lighting. Saver's Switch, a program in existence since October 1, 1991, provides a 15 percent summer energy discount to customers who allow NSP to utilize electricity more efficiently by cycling their central air conditioners on peak days. Further, NSP offers interruptible rate packages that can significantly reduce customer bills.

Managing the peak demand so that electrical service can be provided to all customers every day is another important goal of NSP. The company recently made public its plans to build an $81.5 million combustion turbine facility at the Pathfinder site northeast of Sioux Falls. In January 1992, South Dakota Governor George Mickelson made the exciting announcement.

"This is a major move into South Dakota by a company that is an important part of the energy infrastructure of the upper Midwest," the governor said. "The decision to locate this electrical energy production plant in South Dakota indicates NSP's partnership with Sioux Falls and state officials to share in the economic growth of our state."

"Our commitment to the environment is part of our commitment to the community," says Angus Anson. "We recycle everything, including paper and wood products, and we try to be a community leader in the recycling and energy conservation movement."

The construction of the facility, which consists of two 100-megawatt natural gas or oil-fired combustion turbine units, is in response to increasing demand for electricity throughout the company's five-state service territory. Just 1 megawatt of electricity can service approximately 1,000 residential customers. Ultimately, the Pathfinder site may accommodate a total of four 100-megawatt turbine units.

"Our customers are participating in NSP-sponsored energy saving programs," Anson says. "The combustion turbines in Sioux Falls and our efforts in helping people use energy wisely will allow us to meet customer needs throughout the 1990s."

GROWING WITH SIOUX FALLS

NSP's most recent multimillion dollar commitment to the future is certainly a major step, but the company has always invested heavily in its Sioux Falls operations. Besides annual expenditures just to keep the system going, maintain cable, update services, and add new customer services—a budget item of $5 million in 1992—NSP has recently built a new $1 million substation in the southeastern section of Sioux Falls to help meet electricity needs in one of the community's fastest growing residential areas.

"On average, we're growing faster in Sioux Falls than in the rest of NSP's service area," Anson says. "We've seen a customer increase of over 22 percent in the past 10 years."

According to Anson, that increase is not totally unexpected. NSP-SD works hand-in-hand with the city government in its planning efforts and tries to anticipate growth at least two years in advance. As city planners continue to stretch the boundaries of Sioux Falls, NSP is prepared, planning and extending its service net so that new homes can plug right into dependable, low-cost electrical power.

But providing electricity and aiding in the planning effort is only part of the important role this corporate citizen plays in Sioux Falls. NSP also distributes approximately $200,000 in community support and economic development funds each year and participates in many of the civic organizations which help to maintain a high quality of life in Sioux Falls.

"NSP has been part of the Sioux Falls community for over three-quarters of a century," Anson says. "That gives us a feeling of pride, but it also brings a feeling of responsibility. We want to make sure that we do all we can to make Sioux Falls the kind of place where people want to live—not just today, but well into the 21st century."

NSP-SD Business Operations Manager Jim Wilcox (left) and Construction Manager Russ Bartunek (middle) review customer service plans with General Manager and Chief Executive Angus Anson (right).

A LOT HAS CHANGED IN THE DAIRY INDUSTRY SINCE THE years following World War I when horse-drawn wagons traveled down the cobblestone streets of Sioux Falls, but Lakeside Dairy has made the transition easy by always being a leader. Today, its double-trailer trucks haul hundreds of products every day to customers throughout South Dakota, southwest Minnesota, and northwest Iowa. ◆ The list

of Lakeside's firsts is long. The company was the first in the local market to replace returnable bottles with paper half-gallon cartons. It was also the first to introduce two-pak gallons, the first to offer screw-top plastic gallon jugs, and the first to put tamper-proof freshness seals on all of its products.

In an age of increasing commitment to personal fitness, Lakeside was the first, and only, dairy in South Dakota to introduce a full product line for health-conscious consumers: Tasty, Light &

Creamy. The TLC line includes a complete family of dairy products, from basic milk and cultured products to frozen desserts. The unique line comes in answer to a frequently expressed customer demand.

"Tasty, Light & Creamy is really a big step for us, and for the dairy industry," says Larry Groves, president of Lakeside Dairy. "In the past, consumers have felt that removing fat from dairy products took away some of the taste. But health-conscious dairy lovers

today want the low-fat versions. Tasty, Light & Creamy offers low-fat and low-calorie dairy products with added calcium and protein to enhance the taste.

"People grow up with dairy products. They want to continue to enjoy milk, ice cream, cheese, and other dairy goods even though they know they must decrease their cholesterol and fat intake. We've found a way to let people enjoy the taste of quality dairy products and still be health-conscious."

AN IMPORTANT FORCE IN SIOUX FALLS

Lakeside's tradition of innovation has led the company to statewide leadership in the dairy industry. As South Dakota's largest dairy processor, the company employs over 200 people. Its products are processed through its plant in Sioux Falls, covering the whole range of items in the grocer's dairy case.

For 75 years, Lakeside Dairy has delivered fresh, quality products to the customer's front door.

Lakeside is the only dairy in South Dakota to offer a full product line for health-conscious consumers: Tasty, Light & Creamy.

In an effort to better serve its customers, Lakeside has developed innovative programs for grocery stores and other distribution points that have made it the number one dairy in the state in sales. For example, the company provides a 24-hour, toll-free hotline and offers educational seminars on marketing for its customers. But Lakeside is especially proud of the leadership role it has taken in recycling.

"Obviously, recycling is something we've all got to get involved in," Groves says. "We've established recycling bins at nearly every grocery location in the community, encouraging people to recycle plastic, including, of course, our gallon milk jugs. All proceeds from our recycled plastics program benefit Youth Enrichment Services, a local charity. It's one way we can help the community."

Another Lakeside effort to assist Youth Enrichment Services is the Annual Milk Carton Boat Race at Covell Lake in Terrace Park. Companies, individuals, and civic organizations in Sioux Falls design colorful, original boats made from milk cartons and race them across the mid-town lake. Each year the event draws thousands of spectators and participants who enjoy an afternoon of fun while making a lasting contribution to the community.

In addition to helping Sioux Falls grow, Lakeside recognizes the importance of its own expansion to meet increased market demand. Currently, a modern fleet of over 200 trucks moves products efficiently around the state, some with double trailers. The com-

> In an effort to better serve its customers, Lakeside Dairy has developed innovative programs for grocery stores and other distribution points that have made it the number one dairy in the state in sales.

pany, which continually makes changes and upgrades to improve production and ensure quality, recently added 5,000 square feet of additional cooler space to its Sioux Falls plant.

Groves feels that the food industry has been increasingly aware of the need to maintain the highest possible standards. "We do more," he says. "We are inspected regularly by the FDA and state agencies, and we consistently score well above industry standards. We're proud of that tradition at Lakeside Dairy."

A HERITAGE OF SERVICE
Throughout its history, Lakeside Dairy has remained on the leading edge of customer service in the dairy industry. After 75 years of growth, beginning in 1917, service remains a major element of the Lakeside heritage.

"We've come a long way from the horse-drawn milk wagon," Groves says, "but we haven't forgotten about it. Here in Sioux Falls, we still served some routes by horse-drawn wagons in the '50s. That's one of the reasons we offer home delivery routes even today. It's part of the tradition of service the community has come to expect from Lakeside Dairy—and we're in the business of meeting our customers' needs and expectations."

In an era when packaging and marketing often seem more important than the product itself, it's comforting to know that Lakeside Dairy still delivers fresh, quality products to the customer's front door.

H ENRY CARLSON SR. WAS JUST 18 YEARS OLD WHEN he immigrated to the United States from Sweden in 1902. For the next decade and a half, Carlson worked for the Manchester Biscuit Company and homesteaded for one year in western South Dakota, three miles south of Cottonwood. He later returned to Sioux Falls to work as a construction laborer and to learn the stone mason trade before

establishing the construction company that now bears his name.

The firm was started in 1917 with William A. Snitkey and was incorporated two years later as the Carlson-Snitkey Construction Company. In 1924, Carlson purchased Snitkey's interest, and the company was renamed the Henry Carlson Company. During the '20s and '30s, the firm

A TRADITION OF "HANDS-ON" EXPERIENCE

Three generations of Carlsons have been involved in managing the successful family business over the years, and a tradition of "hands-on" experience, which began with Henry Sr., has continued. Henry Carlson Jr., now president, first worked for the company nearly 50 years ago as a laborer and brick tender

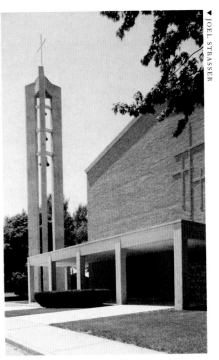

St. Mary's Church is one of the many projects completed over the years by the Henry Carlson Company in Sioux Falls.

The Carlson family has a long history of involvement in the local construction industry. From left: Henry "Chip" III, Henry Sr., and Henry Jr.

worked throughout South Dakota building many of the landmarks still present, such as the Alex-Johnson Hotel and the South Dakota State Cement Plant in Rapid City, and the County Courthouse and Annex to the State Capitol in Pierre.

on an addition to the Manchester Biscuit Company before entering the army in 1943. After World War II was over, Henry Jr. attended the University of Colorado prior to working as superintendent of the Crippled Children's Hospital in Hot Springs, South Dakota. His son, Henry "Chip" Carlson III, began his career working as a carpenter's apprentice before earning a degree in construction management from Northeast Louisiana University. Chip has been active in all phases of manage-

ment, from assistant superintendent to estimating and project management.

The company's founding standards for quality and efficiency have always been its driving force. Because time is such an important factor in the construction industry, the often complicated work schedules must be established far in advance. Over the years, the Henry Carlson Company has earned a reputation for success in meeting deadlines. While speed is critical, quality and permanence are equally important.

"We have a reputation for getting things done that goes back a long way," says Henry Carlson Jr. "Much of that can be attributed to our people, some of whom have been with us for their entire careers. Quality and timeliness are critical in our business, so it's important to have good people who can get the job done. We have the manpower and experience to solve construction problems that other firms

The firm's list of special projects reads like the pages of local history, including Sioux Valley Hospital.

are often unwilling or unable to tackle. We've always been aggressive about going to areas that others aren't familiar with."

LOCAL PROJECTS

It is likely that anyone who lives in or visits Sioux Falls will come in contact with a Henry Carlson Company project. The firm's list of special projects reads like the pages of local history, including the major portion of Washington High School, Sioux Valley Hospital, Veterans Hospital, Minnehaha County Courthouse, the Public Safety Building, the Arena, and many other public and private buildings throughout the city.

Most recently, Henry Carlson Company completed work on the renovation and restoration of the elegant Shoto-Tien Japanese Garden at Terrace Park. "The renovation of the Japanese Garden was a labor of love," Carlson says. "We worked closely with a local garden

group, the city's architect, and a Japanese landscape architect on the master plan. We were responsible for the reshaping of the site: setting large boulders, one at a time, building the arbors, and constructing the exposed aggregate walks that meander through

Recently, Henry Carlson Company completed work on the renovation and restoration of the elegant Shoto-Tien Japanese Garden at Terrace Park.

the grounds and give the garden its distinctive look. It was a small project, but one that is important to the history and future of our community."

According to Carlson, the firm can tackle just about any job. "With our background, we feel confident in our ability to handle the big projects," he says. "For 75 years, we have been bringing the same old-fashioned standards of quality and workmanship to every job we do."

WHEN THE HISTORIC BELL IN THE TOWER OF Old Main rang for the first time in Sioux Falls back in 1918, it was signaling the end of its travels. Since 1869, the bell had followed the westward path of Norwegian immigrants. Dedicated to providing an education for their children in this new world, those pioneers made Augustana a "college on wheels" until its location in Sioux Falls during World War I. Since then, the city and Augustana College have remained cooperative neighbors as the community has grown to surround the campus, once located on the western edge of Sioux Falls.

From its humble, one-structure beginnings as Lutheran Normal School, Augustana College has expanded to a campus of 100 acres and 22 major buildings. Accredited as a four-year liberal arts college by the North Central Association of Colleges and Schools, Augustana is affiliated with the Evangelical Lutheran Church in America. Financial aid is available to promising and qualified students through scholarships, grants, campus work opportunities, and off-campus job listings. Each year, Augustana students share in financial assistance awarded in recognition of academic merit, special talents, and financial need.

AN INVALUABLE COMMUNITY RESOURCE

The longtime partnership that has developed between the college and the city relies on a two-way flow of support and resources. Non-traditional students age 23 or older from Sioux Falls and the surrounding area make up one-fourth of Augustana's 2,000-student enrollment, while adult classes are available year-round for people interested in continuing their education at the college level.

Augustana students are actively involved in the community, too. More than 200 are members of the 15 Augustana Outreach teams which participate in various forms of ministry within a 100-mile radius of the campus. Internship studies conducted in work settings throughout the city enable students to receive hands-on experience in their chosen fields while contributing to the betterment of Sioux Falls.

The community also benefits from access to several Augustana College programs and facilities. The Center for Western Studies sponsors projects and educational programs and is actively involved in the publication of books and manuscripts about the area and its people.

Art lovers can view a variety of student and professional works in the Eide/Dalrymple Gallery, named in memory of beloved Augustana art professors Palmer Eide and Ogden Dalrymple. Works by both men are located around the campus, as well as in private collections around the country. The gallery hosts several exhibits throughout the school year.

Grants from the Van Demark Educational and Charitable Trust created Augustana College's Guy E. Van Demark Lecture Series, which brings notable speakers to the city. Dr. Van Demark, who died in 1983, was a pioneer orthopedic surgeon, an early promoter of rehabilitation programs for the physically handicapped, and the founder of South Dakota's first orthopedic specialty practice.

Mikkelsen Library, located on campus, serves as the hub for an interlibrary courier service that extends throughout South Dakota. Linking 30 libraries across the state, Mikkelsen uses an automated catalog to access holdings for patrons both on and off campus.

In the arena of performance and the arts, Augustana has been a core element of Sioux Falls' growth as a regional fine arts center. Concert choirs and bands from the college have earned international acclaim. Each fall, the Viking Varieties student talent show plays to capacity crowds at the Sioux Falls Coliseum. Christmas Vespers ushers in the holiday season at Augustana with five public appearances that regularly fill local churches. Community participation in the Augustana College/Community Concert Band makes this group one of the area's most popular. With over 90 musicians from Sioux Falls, the surrounding communities, and the college, the ensemble performs two concerts per semester.

Each school year, students are featured in productions from modern drama to classic musical comedy offered by Augustana's Drama Department and staged in the school's Little Theatre. The Shalom Center offers opportunities for continuing theological education on an ecumenical basis, with

From its humble, one-structure beginnings as Lutheran Normal School (above), Augustana College has expanded to a campus of 100 acres and 22 major buildings (opposite).

outreach programs serving South Dakota, Iowa, and Minnesota. Thousands of high school students visit the Augustana College campus annually to participate in science, drama, speech, music, religious, and athletic activities.

As one of two Lutheran colleges with NCAA Division II membership, Augustana also has a proud sports tradition. In Sioux Falls, the Augustana College teams are the "home team" for local sports fans. The Vikings compete in the North Central Conference, considered the premier Division II conference in the nation. Augustana fields men's and women's teams in 16 sports and annually attracts more than 115,000 spectators. The Elmen Center is a modern athletic and wellness facility, anchoring an athletic complex that includes softball and baseball fields, intramural softball diamonds, football practice fields and fieldhouse, and an all-weather track.

A LONGTIME PARTNERSHIP WITH SIOUX FALLS

Clearly, Augustana College has made itself a vital part of Sioux Falls and the region. Over half of Augustana's graduates stay in South Dakota. In fact, nearly 2,500 alumni are currently living and working in Sioux Falls in careers which include law, medicine, education, journalism, aviation, and business. Local Augustana alumni give back generously to the college, volunteering their time and professional experience to work with students who are investigating similar careers.

Keeping an eye on the future is the key to Augustana's growth, college leaders say. Careful planning and a good neighbor policy have brought the college from its wagon wheel days to the present. New buildings are planned for the social sciences and business administration departments of the college, as well as for theatre and fine arts. Amid the progress, the historic bell in Old Main will continue to sound—a link to the past and a symbol of educational excellence to ring out across the Dakota prairie.

I N JUNE 1992, CENTRAL PLAINS CLINIC ENTERED A NEW ERA of medical care when its main clinic moved to a state-of-the-art facility on the campus of McKennan Hospital at 20th Street and Cliff Avenue. The seven-story clinic is the new professional home to a medical staff of more than 90 physicians representing over 35 specialty and subspecialty medical fields. In fact, Central Plains Clinic plays a major role in

The clinic occupied a state-of-the-art facility on the campus of McKennan Hospital in June of 1992.

making Sioux Falls one of the largest subspecialty medical centers in the United States.

The roots of Central Plains Clinic can be traced back nearly 75 years to the general practice of Dr. Stephen A. Donahoe, a pioneering local physician. When Dr. Donahoe established his practice in Sioux Falls in 1915, the growing city on the prairie was home to nearly 19,000 people. Today, the local medical community serves 100,000 residents in Sioux Falls and another quarter million in the surrounding area. Moreover, Sioux Falls is considered the premier medical center between Minneapolis and Denver, and Central Plains

Clinic, the descendent of Dr. Donahoe's practice, is the largest privately owned physician group in South Dakota.

THE DONAHOE CLINIC
The clinic concept itself was introduced in Sioux Falls in 1952 by Dr. Jack Donahoe, Stephen Donahoe's son. Jack Donahoe had completed his residency at the renowned Mayo Clinic in Rochester, Minnesota, when he returned to Sioux Falls to practice internal medicine with his father and his brother, Bob Donahoe. He convinced them that a modern clinic, a partnership among the doctors

personnel, as well as exchange information and gain from each other's individual areas of expertise. The clinic would operate independently, allowing its physicians to treat patients at any area hospital or medical facility.

The Donahoe Clinic, as the partnership was originally called, opened in the National Bank of South Dakota building (now the Western Bank Building) in downtown Sioux Falls at Ninth and Phillips streets. Original partners included the three Donahoes; Dr. Russell Orr, obstetrics and gynecology; and Dr. Jeff Cottum, surgeon. Later staff additions included Dr. Robert Nelson, surgeon; Dr. Vincent Cutshall and Dr. Michael Ferrell, internists; Dr. Vernon Cutshall and Dr. Edward Peters, family practitioners; and Dr. Richard Hosen, pediatrician.

RELOCATION AND EXPANSION
The clinic quickly outgrew the space in the bank building and in 1954 relocated to a facility at 23rd Street and South Minnesota Avenue, near what was then the southern edge of the city. As the clinic continued to grow, so did its reputation for quality medical care, attracting more physicians with specialties and subspecialties that were new to the Sioux Falls area. By the mid-1970s, over 25 doctors were doubling up on office space at the clinic in south Sioux Falls.

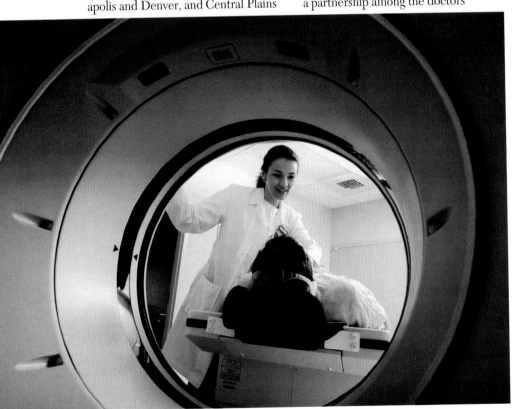

Central Plains Clinic offers new services and equipment at the main clinic, including a CT scanner in the radiology department.

working in the area, could be successful in Sioux Falls.

The advantages of a partnership were numerous. Most importantly, the partners could share specialized equipment, supplies, and administrative

Today, Central Plains Clinic perpetuates its founding commitment to health care that is convenient, comprehensive, and personal.

When the clinic relocated again in 1976, the group changed its name to Central Plains Clinic. A new 66,000-square-foot building was constructed on a 17-acre campus on South Kiwanis Avenue at 34th Street. Originally housing 40 doctors, the clinic quickly outgrew yet another location. When the facility was finally expanded in 1986, the partnership had grown to 60 physicians.

In 1985, Central Plains Clinic opened its first family practice satellite facility. Central Plains Clinic East today has five family practice physicians and one specializing in geriatrics. It also has routine radiology and laboratory facilities, as well as an optometrist and optical shop.

As the main clinic continued to add physicians and services, it soon needed a new and larger medical building, one that would provide the most up-to-date medical services and technology to the thousands of patients who were visiting the Central Plains Clinic annually. The logical answer to the clinic's future needs was the recently constructed medical building on the McKennan Hospital campus at 20th Street and Cliff Avenue.

A more efficient facility with space to accommodate future growth, the main clinic offers new services and

equipment, such as a CT scanner in the radiology department, increased laboratory facilities, a state-of-the-art information system, two adjacent parking ramps, a valet parking service, a deli, and a health store.

"Our goal at Central Plains Clinic has always been quality care," says Edward Arshem, clinic administrator. "We know we can continue that tradition and make further advances in our new facility."

The new location in central Sioux Falls is also more convenient to a greater number of patients and to area hospitals. Likewise, clinic patients have the added convenience of a sheltered free parking facility that is connected by skywalk to the clinic. A new valet parking service is also available at no charge.

Despite its move to new quarters, Central Plains Clinic retained the medical facility on South Kiwanis Avenue, which now operates as Central Plains Clinic West. Five family practice physicians, a specialist in geriatrics, a pediatric after-hours clinic, an optometrist,

and an optical shop continue to meet patient needs at that location. The Acute Care Clinic is also housed at the west facility, as are X-ray and routine laboratory services.

AN EYE TO THE FUTURE

As the medical needs of the Sioux Falls area and region continue to grow, and as technology advances and medical knowledge increases, Central Plains Clinic strives to meet the challenges of the present with an eye to the future.

"Although the medical world is vastly changed since the days when Dr. Stephen Donahoe started his practice and when the group started the first clinic in the city, the Central Plains Clinic operates on some of the same important principles," says Arshem. "Our pledge is to ensure that the health care delivered here is the finest anywhere, to provide our staff and our patients with the latest medical technology available, and to make certain that access to health care is convenient, comprehensive, and personal. That's a pledge Dr. Donahoe believed in too."

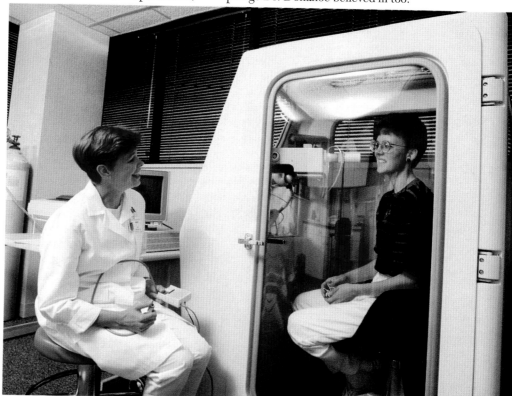

The clinic's medical staff of more than 90 physicians represents over 35 specialty and subspecialty medical fields.

IN 1924, WHEN B.O. STORDAHL AND LLOYD WAGGONER founded the law firm that would become May, Johnson, Doyle & Becker, P.C., they had no idea what a unique organization they were starting. Throughout its rich history in Sioux Falls, the firm has attracted a host of standouts in the legal profession, including a nationally recognized expert in motor carrier and public utility law, a South Dakota governor,

and one of the youngest U.S. Attorneys in history.

Robert G. May joined founders Stordahl and Waggoner in 1939, and became a partner in the firm after Waggoner's death. During and after World War II, May, who is currently "of counsel" to the firm, emerged as one of the country's leading attorneys in the field of public utility and motor carrier law.

In 1945, after serving as a naval officer during the war, Nils Boe joined the firm, which became known as Stordahl, May & Boe. He was elected

Boe was appointed as a federal judge on what is now the United States Court of International Trade, assuming senior status in 1984. Following his federal appointments, he withdrew from the firm.

George O. Johnson, now also "of counsel," became a partner in 1960, and the firm changed its name once again to Stordahl, May, Boe & Johnson.

Harold C. (Bud) Doyle was appointed U.S. Attorney for South Dakota by President John F. Kennedy in 1961. After leaving that post in 1969, he joined the firm and has since developed

In 1979, the firm underwent its final name change to May, Johnson, Doyle & Becker, P.C. A full-service legal practice, the firm also includes principals Derald W. Wiehl, who practices in civil litigation; Richard Moe, who concentrates in corporate law, federal income, estate and gift taxation, and estate planning; Lon J. Kouri, who focuses on civil litigation and construction law; Jeffrey D. Brekke, practicing in the areas of estate planning, commercial, business, and real estate law; and Richard L. Travis, who concentrates on civil litigation and commercial and criminal law. Also associated with the firm are Martin Oyos, editor in chief of the South Dakota Law Review (1987-88), and Terry G. Westergaard.

BLAZING A TRAIL IN SIOUX FALLS

After nearly 70 years in and near downtown Sioux Falls, May, Johnson, Doyle & Becker has built a new office facility, blazing a trail in suburban Sioux Falls. The firm's modern, 13,400-square-foot facility at 57th Street and Minnesota Avenue was occupied in the fall of 1992. According to principal Jim Becker, moving away from the city's center was a difficult choice. Ultimately, convenience was the deciding factor.

"We wanted maximum convenience for clients coming to our office," Becker says, "with plenty of parking and easy access. The corner of 57th and Minnesota is increasingly a part of people's traffic patterns, and we wanted to be able to grow as Sioux Falls grows."

The new facility gives May, Johnson, Doyle & Becker the flexibility to add additional attorneys, develop a growing client base, and expand the current support staff to meet the rapidly changing needs of the firm's clients.

"A location like this is not unusual in Minneapolis or Chicago," Becker says, "but it's a new idea in Sioux Falls to move to a suburban location. We feel that we're blazing a trail and leading the way into a new area. It's yet another exciting step for our firm—just one more element in a history of being unique among our community's law practices."

From left: The firm's principals are Richard L. Travis, Derald W. Wiehl, Jeffrey D. Brekke, James R. Becker, Harold C. Doyle, Lon J. Kouri, and Richard Moe.

to the state legislature for four terms from 1951 to 1959 and served as speaker of the house. After his election as lieutenant governor in 1963, Boe was elected governor of South Dakota for two terms, serving from 1965 to 1969. He was later named director of the Office of Intergovernmental Relations and assistant director of the Office of Emergency Preparedness of the White House by President Nixon. In 1971,

a reputation as a trial lawyer and mediator. Doyle is also a member of the U.S. Mediation and Arbitration Service.

James R. Becker joined the firm in 1963 after receiving his law degree from the University of Minnesota. Practicing in the areas of estate planning/probate and general business and corporation law, including qualified retirement plans and employment discrimination, Becker is also a member of the American Arbitration Association. Together, Becker and Doyle bring to the firm a level of expertise in arbitration and mediation that is unique in Sioux Falls.

IT WAS A SIMPLER TIME IN A YOUNG BUT GROWING SIOUX Falls when George Sercl Sr. opened a grocery store at the corner of 10th and Phillips in 1931 and named it the Sunshine Food Market. In those days, he could not have envisioned that his neighborhood market would be the beginning of a shopping tradition for generations of Sioux Falls area residents. Today, 60 years after Sercl got his start, there are six Sunshine Food Markets in the city, one store in Yankton, and another in Mitchell.

The stores' bright yellow signs featuring a smiling sun are familiar landmarks in the neighborhoods they serve—friendly symbols of the helpful service that customers find inside. That's because, to its founder, Sunshine was more than just a store; it was a personal commitment to genuinely serve the customer. George Sercl himself summed it up in just three words: "Service, Savings, and Satisfaction."

What made it even more important to live up to those words was the fact that most of Sercl's early customers were his neighbors and friends. The founder wanted them to consider Sunshine their "hometown store." That type of community pride and commitment to meeting customers' needs has brought in four generations of Sioux Falls residents to shop at Sunshine Food Markets.

TRADITION AND CHANGE

"While we've always kept pace with changes in the grocery business, we have also held fast to our tradition of providing 'Service, Savings, and Satisfaction,' and we're proud of that," says George Sercl Jr., son of the founder and current Sunshine president. Sercl Jr. continues the family ownership of Sunshine, along with two of his children who also work for the company.

Other important things about Sunshine haven't changed, including the big smiles and the hearty meals served up at Sunshine's cafes, which continue to serve as neighborhood gathering spots from breakfast-time to the afternoon coffee break. For thousands of Sioux Falls children, Sandy the mechanical horse remains synonymous with Sunshine. Located at each store's entrance, Sandy has provided many hours of adventure over the years for just a penny a ride.

The years have brought change, but always with the goal of better serving customers. Sunshine has put particular emphasis in recent years on making shopping more convenient for busier lifestyles. Today, newer and remodeled stores each have their own in-store delis and bakeries. In addition, three Sioux Falls Sunshine locations are open 24 hours a day to accommodate a full range of work schedules and lifestyles.

With the convenience of customers in mind, the company today builds larger stores to stock more merchandise and offer greater selection among products. The two newest Sunshine Food Markets are the East 10th Street store, opened in 1987, and the West 10th and Kiwanis store, opened in 1990. In addition, the 41st Street store was expanded and remodeled in 1990.

"We've grown up along with Sioux Falls and our customers," says Sercl Jr. "We're proud that Sunshine Food Markets are a part of Sioux Falls and the spirit of independent business that thrives here. My father believed in that, and all of us at Sunshine still do."

Sunshine Food Markets and Sioux Falls have been growing together since 1931. Today, George Sercl Jr. (above) serves as president of the company his father founded.

A CORPS OF 1,000 PROFESSIONAL DRIVERS DEDICATED to service and safety is the key to success for Midwest Coast Transport—a Sioux Falls company that hauls an alphabet of goods for some of America's best-known businesses. ♦ "Our company has an unusual structure for a trucking business," says Murray Smith, MCT president. "We run hundreds of trucks, but the company doesn't own a

single power unit—the motorized tractor that pulls the trailer. Independent contractors called owner-operators lease their trucks to us, and we arrange the loads with our customers across the nation. The owner-operators we hire log over 90 million miles annually while pulling MCT's 1,200 trailers."

Making this complex delivery system successful on a day-to-day basis requires a 150-person staff at the Sioux Falls headquarters, a highly sophisticated computer system, and some luck. "MCT people are the best in the business and the most important part of the equation," Smith says. "But sometimes you've got to have a little luck— like good weather, a load that's ready to go on time, or just a clear road ahead."

EFFICIENCY, SAFETY, RELIABILITY

The company was founded in Sioux Falls in 1949 to transport goods for two large local clients: John Morrell & Co., a meat products company, and Nash Finch, a grocery wholesaler. MCT still hauls for its first two customers, but ownership changed hands in 1989 to several Sioux Falls residents. The business has also expanded considerably in recent years by adding many tractors, trailers, and drivers to the fleet.

Many of the company's major customers operated their own trucking fleets until they were convinced that a professional transportation firm could do a better job. Through an efficient Operations Department, MCT trucks

"MCT people are the best in the business and the most important part of the equation," says Murray Smith, president.

waste very little time on the road. For example, an operator might haul a load of movie film from Minnesota to Hollywood, pick up a shipment of retail merchandise from a California manufacturer and haul it to New Jersey, reload candy destined for Florida, then haul a load of houseplants to Wisconsin.

Since its founding in 1949, MCT has grown from a local operation to a major transportation company delivering products nationwide to businesses, hospitals, and schools.

MCT operators are more than efficient; they are also safe and reliable. The company received the Carrier of the Year Award from Target Stores, 3M Company, and Oscar Mayer Foods Corp. from 1988 to 1991, and from Nabisco Brands, Inc. in 1989 and 1990. MCT also has won numerous state and regional safety awards.

QUALIFYING QUALITY DRIVERS

Qualifying quality drivers is the key to safety and reliability. Since 1973, the company has operated a driver's school that has trained over 3,500 men and women to be highly professional over-the-road drivers for MCT and other companies that run their own fleets. About two-thirds of MCT's drivers and owner-operators are graduates of the program.

It's a profession that's not for everyone, but it's a good one for self-motivated, entrepreneurial people. "Individuals with no specific educational background who really want to get ahead can come to our school, learn to drive, and be making a good living in a short time," explains Duane Odland, vice president of safety and fleet administration. "We require our student drivers to put in 50,000 miles with a lead driver, learn company policy, work with customers, and become true professionals."

MCT also has a program that helps its drivers buy their own power units. That step—becoming an owner-operator leased to MCT—is often the beginning of a major business as a fleet owner. In fact, almost all of the firm's fleet owners today started out with one truck, solid proof of the excellent career opportunities MCT offers.

The company has many second- and third-generation drivers and several husband-and-wife teams; of its 1,000 drivers, over 100 are women. Though many MCT drivers live in Sioux Falls, others are based in cities and communities all over the United States. And a number of recent U.S. immigrants have pursued the American dream by enrolling in the MCT driving school.

Each year, owner-operators log over 90 million miles while pulling MCT's 1,200 trailers. Dedicated to safety and service, this corps of 1,000 professional drivers transports everything from houseplants to movie film.

"We've had several Soviets go through our program," says Odland. "Recently, a man from Czechoslovakia began driving for one of MCT's fleet operators. He's a hard worker and is saving as much money as he can—over $7,000 so far—to buy his own truck so that he can bring other members of his family over from the former Czechoslovakia."

NATIONWIDE SUCCESS

MCT has grown from a local operation hauling just meat and potatoes to a major transportation company delivering products nationwide to businesses, hospitals, and schools. As one of the state's largest employers, MCT has an additional impact on the local economy by purchasing over $3 million in equipment and supplies annually.

"We are successful because we offer safe, efficient, and professional transportation services that meet or exceed our customers' expectations," says Smith. "We provide excellent training, a good income, and opportunities for career advancement to our drivers who are clearly the backbone of the company."

AT THE EXPANSIVE 17-ACRE YARD AT EGGER STEEL Company, welded plate girder bridge beams lie side by side, waiting to be shipped to the job site. During the fabricating process, they are transformed from steel plates shipped from producing mills into bridge beams for use by contractors in improving the country's infrastructure. The fabricating process involves highly skilled workmanship,

adhering to various codes and specifications. Egger's 50 administrative, sales, and engineering personnel and its 100 dedicated shop employees are keenly aware of the responsibility that goes along with their work.

Three weathering steel canopies frame the entry way to the firm's offices.

"We've always prided ourselves on the quality of our work," says Steve Egger, company president. "We work in an inspection environment on a daily basis. Our own highly skilled quality control team works right alongside inspectors from state departments of transportation and testing agencies."

Producing a quality product has been the goal of Egger Steel Company since Albert Egger and George Scudder founded the firm in 1946. Steve Egger, son of Albert Egger, joined the business in 1971 and became president in 1976. "Our biggest challenge is to keep up with the changing times," Egger says. "For example, until just a few years ago, most bridge beams were delivered to contractors with a simple prime coat of paint. Today, almost all state D.O.T. specifications call for the finish coat of paint to be applied in the fabricator's shop."

Egger Steel Company strives to incorporate a change of this type into its business by bringing management and employees together to solve problems.

This team approach was used in 1991 to remodel the company's existing paint shop, enabling more bridge girders to be processed simultaneously. "Sooner or later, all steel companies that wish to be in the bridge fabricating business will have to adopt this kind of painting technology," says Doug Johnson, executive vice president and general manager.

THREE BUSINESS COMPONENTS

Egger Steel Company is divided into three distinct business components. The contract structural division provides fabricated structural steel to general contractors on building projects throughout the region, with an emphasis on state and local projects. This division strives to offer a complete steel package, including fabricated structural and miscellaneous steel, reinforcing steel, steel joists, metal decks, and metal specialty items. Recent Sioux Falls projects include the new Roosevelt and Washington high schools, Central Plains Clinic, and the Commerce Center. Egger has also supplied the structural steel for two decades worth of expansions at Sioux Valley Hospital and McKennan Hospital. The Cultural Heritage Center in Pierre, Frost Arena in Brookings, and Rapid City Regional Hospital are just a few of the major building projects across the state for which the firm has provided the steel.

The bridge structural division supplies fabricated structural steel for bridges in a 10-state region. Welded plate girder and wide flange bridge beams fabricated at Egger Steel Company are in use in bridges in South Dakota, North Dakota, Minnesota, Iowa, Wyoming, Montana, Colorado, Nebraska, Kansas, and New Mexico. According to Steve Egger, working in so many states is particularly challenging, as each state department of trans-

portation has its own set of specifications. Bridge beams up to 120 feet long weighing as much as 30 tons are regularly shipped on Egger trucks to job sites throughout the region.

The steel service center is Egger Steel Company's contact with the greatest number of customers in the region. The service center supplies plain and preprocessed material to a variety of customers ranging from small welding and repair shops to many of the area's largest manufacturing concerns. The service center stocks a complete line of carbon steel products with an emphasis on customer service and timely delivery of materials. Processing services performed include sawing to length, plate burning, shearing, rolling, and breaking.

Each year, Egger Steel Company handles 15,000 to 18,000 tons of steel, the majority of which is received via railcar. The company maintains its own fleet of semi tractors and trailers and employs its own drivers to provide the best possible delivery to customers.

Steve Egger considers the team management approach the real key to the company's success. In fact, many loyal employees have spent their entire careers in the positive work environment at Egger Steel Company.

Trains roll in daily to the Egger Steel yard with new material to be fabricated and processed, while trucks are loaded to deliver the finished product to the job site. Inside, sparks

The nursing tower at Sioux Valley Hospital features a structural steel frame fabricated in Egger's shops.

fly from the welders, and overhead cranes keep the steel moving, helping build Sioux Falls and the region and creating a secure infrastructure for the future.

ONE OF THE GREATEST MEMORIES AT SWEETMAN Const. Co., according to company President Merle Davis, is the public acclaim which arose from the firm's 1984 reconstruction of Minnesota Avenue — at the time, the busiest road in South Dakota. "People couldn't believe how quickly it was finished," Davis says. "We moved on that project so fast it hardly disrupted the flow of traffic."

The Benson Road Interchange, completed in 1992, was a Sweetman project from start to finish.

Since its founding in 1952, this local company has been growing right along with Sioux Falls. Today, Sweetman Const. Co. is often called on to supply rock, sand, gravel, concrete, and asphalt, and in many cases to build and rebuild the streets that, day after day, carry children to school and their parents to work. For example, the Benson Road Interchange, which opened a new corridor on the northern industrial edge of the city upon its completion in 1992, was a Sweetman project from start to finish.

> **"Our entire company is ready to go the extra mile to make things work for the public," says Merle Davis, company president.**

Concrete Materials, a division of Sweetman Const. Co., supplied the base gravel, concrete, and asphalt to the Benson Road project. The division has its own quartzite rock quarry, sand plants, gravel pits, and ready-mix concrete and asphalt plants in the Sioux Falls area.

"People don't often get a chance to see the steps involved in such a major undertaking," Davis says. "With the Benson Road Interchange, the residents of Sioux Falls saw everything from the engineering to the actual construction of the interchange. It was a big job."

But creating a thoroughfare where only cornfields existed before is business as usual for Sweetman Const. Co. With every new project, the firm faces the usual challenges, such as transporting the tons of material required for building a concrete road or completing an asphalt and rock resurface. In 1989, the company answered that challenge when it acquired a portion of the abandoned Chicago and Northwestern rail line around Sioux Falls. The purchase allows Sweetman to move rock and sand from its quarries by rail, rather than by truck, increasing safety and decreasing wear on city streets and county roads.

According to Chairman of the Board R.C. Sweetman, both are important to the company. "Our concerns are the public's concerns," says Sweetman. "We work for the public and with the public—that's our job."

SERVING SIOUX FALLS AND BEYOND

While Sioux Falls has been the headquarters and heart of Sweetman Const. Co. since 1952, the firm does work for clients throughout South Dakota and in neighboring states. The distinctive Sioux Quartzite quarried locally by Sweetman finds its way all over the country.

"We ship material as far away as Georgia," says Davis. "Quartzite is such a durable and beautiful stone; it's used for everything from architectural panels to roads. We get it right here in Sioux Falls in our quarry near the Sioux Empire Fairgrounds."

Davis adds, "Our entire company is ready to go the extra mile to make things work for the public. People aren't always aware of the many safety considerations involved in our projects, but we certainly are. As we follow the fast pace of growth in Sioux Falls and the surrounding areas, we will strive to make each new project our very best."

Ellis & Eastern, a Sweetman subsidiary, moves construction materials across Sioux Falls.

THE EVANGELICAL LUTHERAN GOOD SAMARITAN Society, a national organization based in Sioux Falls, serves 25,000 elderly people in 26 states through a variety of care and residential facilities. Though it is a success story in worldly terms, the Society today is still driven by the legacy of its founder, the Reverend August Hoeger, who was not only a pioneer in the field of geriatrics, but also a man of vision, determination, and energy. Rev. Hoeger established the Society in the small prairie community of Arthur, North Dakota in 1922. The first Good Samaritan home was a six-room rented house that served primarily physically and mentally handicapped persons, but the Society soon expanded its services to meet the needs of the aged and infirm. By 1930, the demands of the Society were so great that Rev. Hoeger resigned from his congregations and became the full-time head of the Society. That year he also moved both his family and the Society headquarters to Fargo, North Dakota, a more accessible location.

The Society continued to grow under his leadership—by 1940 there were 28 facilities in 10 states—but the organization was not immune to the effects of the Depression. The Society's board of directors voted in 1940 to split the organization into two bodies, and Rev. Hoeger was left with the smaller group of only four facilities, which continued to operate under the organization's original name.

Fueled by Rev. Hoeger's determination, the Society soon recovered and took up its rapid pace of growth again. Today the Society operates 210 Good Samaritan facilities and employs 17,500 people. A religious, charitable, non-profit organization, the Society is also an affiliated social ministry organization of the two major Lutheran Church organizations in the United States: the Evangelical Lutheran Church in America and The Lutheran Church, Missouri Synod.

COMING TO SIOUX FALLS

In 1963, the Society moved its headquarters to Sioux Falls, where it was still operating a Good Samaritan facility established in 1937. In 1970, the year of Rev. Hoeger's death, the Central Office at 1000 West Avenue North was dedicated. Today, there are three care and residential facilities in Sioux Falls: the original Good Samaritan Center, with 141 nursing beds; Good Samaritan Luther Manor, with 118 nursing beds; and Good Samaritan Village, a complex of 150 nursing beds, 72 assisted living beds, and 68 apartments and duplexes.

The Society operates under the leadership of president Mark Jerstad, who joined the organization in 1985. "The Evangelical Lutheran Good Samaritan Society has a mission to share God's love in word and deed by providing shelter and supportive services to older persons and others in need," Jerstad says. "We work very hard to be true to our motto, 'In Christ's Love, Everyone is Someone.'"

The Society's Central Office assists Good Samaritan facilities throughout the country by providing accounting and data processing services, guidance of regional directors, and consulting services in areas such as activities, social services, spiritual ministries, nursing

Top: The Evangelical Lutheran Good Samaritan Society is headquartered at 1000 West Avenue North in Sioux Falls.

Bottom: Good Samaritan Luther Manor, one of the Society's three local care and residential facilities, boasts 118 nursing beds.

GENE'S STUDIO

GENE'S STUDIO

services, architectural design and construction supervision, medical records, environmental services, resource development and public relations, purchasing, and printing.

THE GOOD SAMARITAN LIFE

At each Good Samaritan facility a team of caring professionals works to provide the best possible care for each resident. Individualized plans emphasize the care of the whole person, considering social, spiritual, and emotional needs, as well as physical well-being. A Care Team, comprised of staff members from various disciplines, meets regularly with each resident and his or her family to ensure that the plan of care continues to meet the resident's needs.

In addition to nursing services, many facilities offer a choice of independent living accommodations. Residents may come and go as they wish, entertain guests, and participate in the activities of the center or the community—with the security of knowing immediate assistance is always available through the center's health care staff.

Most importantly, says Jerstad, the Good Samaritan Society offers residents a home in a supportive environment where their needs can be met and they can enjoy contact with persons of similar backgrounds and interests. Good Samaritan centers also offer planning services prior to an individual's admission to diminish the anxiety which

may accompany the move to a nursing home or retirement complex and to make the transition to a new setting as easy as possible.

A CARING TRADITION

The Evangelical Lutheran Good Samaritan Society attributes much of the success of its programs, facilities, and organization to the dynamic ideas of the late Rev. Hoeger, referred to as "Dad" Hoeger by Society staff and friends. "Dad Hoeger established new concepts in care that have become the standard of the elderly care industry nationwide," Jerstad says. "So much of what we take for granted today, such as senior citizens centers, improved resident facilities, and the 'center' concept itself—a residence facility where the medical, physical, social, cultural, and religious needs of an individual are met—were at one time just part of his vision of what could be."

Rev. Hoeger also had the ability to inspire local people to respond to the needs of the elderly in their own communities. Says Jerstad, "In a very real sense, our centers belong to the communities, and we are grateful for the support, volunteer activity, and prayers provided by our advisory boards and other members of our communities."

From the Eagle Scout who builds a walking path complete with benches on the grounds of a center, to the senior citizen from the community who visits weekly to play the "good old songs" on the piano for residents, volunteers are drawn to the Good Samaritan Society.

The Society also sponsors outreach programs to encourage community involvement and interaction with the elderly who are living in their own homes. An example is the Senior Companion Program in Sioux Falls: citizens who are over 62 years old regularly visit those in need to help with meal preparation, shopping, tidying the house—and to just be a friend.

The vision that inspired the lifelong efforts of Rev. Hoeger still guides The Evangelical Lutheran Good Samaritan Society. This Sioux Falls-based national organization continues to make the daily lives of thousands of elderly people more enjoyable and meaningful.

The Society also operates Good Samaritan Village (top), a complex of 150 nursing beds, 72 assisted living beds, and 68 apartments and duplexes, and Good Samaritan Center (bottom), which offers 141 nursing beds.

AT CULBERT-DAVIS CO., "OUTSTANDING SERVICE" IS A company policy that never goes out of style. Since 1959 when the insurance firm was founded, personal attention and service have been its highest priorities. ◆ A medium-size firm with 27 employees, Culbert-Davis Co. is a perfect blend of small agency service excellence and large agency professionalism. "We're small enough to remember your

name when you walk in the door, yet large enough to offer the services you need and expect," says John Knudtson, president. "We've also been in business long enough to know the insurance industry inside out."

John Knudtson, Nick Gusso, and Don Oyen, who have been longtime employees of Culbert-Davis Co., and Brad Messerli purchased the company in 1985 from founders Richard Culbert and Donald Davis. Over the past sev-

suits his or her personal, commercial, or professional needs," Knudtson says. "This is an important aspect of our personalized service."

Another service highlight is the fact that Culbert-Davis Co. is one of the few independent insurance agencies in the region with a department dedicated solely to handling claims. The firm's expertise in combination with today's communications technology guarantees that a claim will be filed at the client's

determine needs and special situations in every aspect of the company's operations. Each business is different. Because we work with so many insurance companies, we can find the appropriate coverage at the lowest possible cost."

The firm's principals are (from left) Nick Gusso, Don Oyen, John Knudtson, and Brad Messerli.

Culbert-Davis Co. also has more than 30 years of experience in providing personal insurance programs for individuals. A broad range of coverage is offered, including homeowner and automobile insurance, umbrella liability policies, life insurance, and personal property coverage for jewelry, fine art, and other valuables. In addition, the personal risk managers at Culbert-Davis Co. can analyze a client's needs and develop a plan of personal insurance designed to provide protection from serious financial setbacks.

FLEXIBILITY FOR THE FUTURE

While the majority of the firm's clients are in the Sioux Falls area and a five-state region, Culbert-Davis Co. is licensed to provide insurance coverage in most states. This flexibility is a necessity for some of the firm's clients. Explains Knudtson, "A client may have their headquarters company in Sioux Falls, a manufacturing plant in Omaha, and a distribution center in Phoenix. We are able to handle insurance needs on all those facilities."

As the firm reflects on its past success, Culbert-Davis Co. is committed to a plan for the future: to maintain the service that has become its trademark. "We're never going to compromise on our after-the-sale service," Knudtson says. "Service is the heart of our business—and it will remain first and foremost in the future of our company."

Culbert-Davis Co. is headquartered on South Cliff Avenue in Sioux Falls.

eral years, the agency's business volume and staff have doubled in size. In 1989, the company moved into a new headquarters building with 6,500 square feet of modern office space at 600 South Cliff Avenue.

AN INDEPENDENT INSURANCE AGENCY

Because Culbert-Davis Co. is an independent property and casualty insurance agency, the staff has the freedom to recognize the individuality of each client when choosing from more than 20 insurance companies. "We roll up our sleeves and work with each client to find the insurance coverage that best

insurance company immediately after it is reported to Culbert-Davis Co. In many instances, Culbert-Davis Co. also has draft authority to make prompt payment of claims, which is another great advantage for the firm's clients.

While Culbert-Davis Co. writes insurance coverage of all kinds, it specializes in commercial insurance needs, from medical malpractice to contractor's insurance and from contract surety bonds to manufacturing risks. Businesses of every size, from the smallest mom-and-pop store to a multi-unit hotel/motel chain, use Culbert-Davis Co. for their insurance needs.

"When a new or an established business comes to us for help in structuring an insurance package," Knudtson says, "we take the time to

MᶜGLADREY & PULLEN OFFERS A UNIQUE RESOURCE to its clients: a national firm with a strong local presence. A CPA and consulting firm established in Sioux Falls in 1960, McGladrey & Pullen's express mission is to provide quality, objective accounting, tax, and consulting services to small and middle-market businesses and their owners. ◆ "We offer the best of both worlds,"

says Dan Hylland, partner in charge of the office. "As a national firm, we have the capacity to provide the services and products business owners need most as their companies grow. Yet, being anchored in Sioux Falls, we can provide clients with the kind of service they expect to receive from a local firm."

PROACTIVE SERVICE

A major objective of McGladrey & Pullen is to provide continuous proactive contact with clients. "We intend to have frequent contact with our clients allowing them the opportunity to use us as a sounding board for their ideas and problems," says Hylland.

Besides having partners accountable and accessible, Deane Teut, a partner in the firm, suggests clients can gauge the service they are getting by whether the firm listens and asks the right questions, anticipates client needs, volunteers information, identifies problems, offers creative, alternative solutions, and goes beyond the routine.

"You can't be just bean counters anymore," Teut says. "Business owners want a partner in their business, someone who gives them objective, sound advice and counsel throughout the year."

TEAM APPROACH

To ensure service and results, McGladrey & Pullen uses an integrated team approach to client engagements. When a client service team is assigned, professionals are matched by their experience in helping clients in similar size businesses and by industry expertise. McGladrey's Sioux Falls professionals have experience in virtually every industry, with particular strengths in the following:
- manufacturing
- banking/thrifts
- health care
- construction

The partners also have direct client service responsibilities. "Clients get frustrated when they want to talk to the partner in charge of their engagement, but the partner is nowhere to be found," explains Hylland. "McGladrey & Pullen is structured so that clients receive a very high amount of partner attention and involvement."

FULL-TIME TAX SPECIALISTS

Because today's tax laws and regulations are so complex, finding a tax specialist who devotes full time to dealing with those issues is extremely important. McGladrey's clients have a partner, manager, and several staff members who dedicate all of their time to helping clients minimize their income tax liabilities.

CONSULTING SERVICES

Providing a broad range of services is another important component in what an accounting firm can do for its clients. In addition to traditional services—audit, accounting, and tax preparation—McGladrey & Pullen offers future-oriented services.

Each day, business owners have to make many decisions dealing with complex issues. McGladrey's consultants help the owner/manager get a grip on the everyday business issues with assistance in the areas of human resources, budgeting, cash flow projections, strategic and business planning, and efficient use of microcomputer, minicomputer, and mainframe software and hardware.

But having a wealth of resources at hand does not translate into premium fees. McGladrey & Pullen's management structure keeps costs under control, and clients are never asked to pay for services they do not need.

"There's a misconception that large means expensive," Hylland says. "Like any other service or product, accounting firms can only charge what the market will bear. Fees in this area are competitive. What our clients are looking for is service: What value can this firm provide that the others can't? And chemistry: Can I work with these people?"

INTERNATIONAL CAPABILITIES

"We see more and more of our clients expanding sales in foreign markets," says Hylland.

To serve their growing needs, McGladrey has an international affiliate that is represented in over 60 countries, bringing clients in-depth knowledge and an understanding of foreign business customs, tax, and regulatory matters.

▲ GENE'S STUDIO

From left: Partners Dale Lien, Dan Hylland, Steve Trapp, and Deane Teut look forward to helping clients maximize their business opportunities in the future.

McGladrey & Pullen also believes in supporting the local community. During the firm's three decades in Sioux Falls, the partners and staff have been active in a variety of civic, charitable, business, and professional organizations.

McGladrey & Pullen has a strong commitment to the local business and civic communities. The partners and staff look forward to being a leader in helping Sioux Falls maintain its reputation as "A Good Thing Going."

OUNDED 25 YEARS AGO, FIEGEN CONSTRUCTION CO. is a family owned and operated business with a reputation for quality, on-time performance, and innovation. A midsize Sioux Falls general contractor with six office employees and some 40 field workers at the height of the construction season, Fiegen nonetheless handles the big and the small, from a $10 million project to an office remodeling job.

"We have capabilities to perform and complete any project in the Sioux Falls area," says founder Ron Fiegen. "What makes our company special is the quality workmanship and personal attention we bring to each project."

Today, Ron Fiegen (center) and his two sons, Jeff and Rusty, share management responsibilities for the 25-year-old family business.

EXPERIENCE IN THE FIELD

Ron Fiegen left the Sioux Falls area as a young man for a career as an iron worker. He advanced quickly to supervisory positions in steel erecting and heavy rigging operations, working on the construction of skyscrapers and major bridges throughout the United States. In 1967, at age 32, he brought his expertise back to his home state and started his own steel erecting business.

Ten years later, Fiegen's company had evolved into a general contracting firm with a specialty in commercial buildings. Today, Ron Fiegen is assisted in the management of the company by his two sons, Jeff and Rusty, who serve as vice presidents. Although both sons have degrees in architectural and civil drafting, they earned their positions in the company

through field experience as welders, concrete finishers, and carpenters.

Over the years, Fiegen has been involved in the construction of some of the city's best known commercial and public facilities, including the Western Banks, the Youth Enrichment Services building, and the new Sioux Falls Armory at the South Dakota National Guard base. The company's list of regional projects includes the Toshiba plant in Mitchell, South Dakota, and the Schwan Sales Enterprises facilities in Marshall, Minnesota.

Fiegen has also developed a reputation for quality construction of churches and schools. In Sioux Falls, the company built the award-winning Church of the Holy Spirit, the library at the North American Baptist Seminary, and the additions to Our Savior Lutheran Church and Peace Lutheran Church. Fiegen Construction also built Madison Middle School in Madison, South Dakota, Southeast Area Vocational Technical School, and Sioux Vocational School for the Handicapped.

FIEGEN INNOVATION

Fiegen Construction is an area leader in two new specialties of the construction industry: design-build and construction management. These areas of expertise are growing in popularity because they save money and time and ensure quality control for the owner.

In the design-build capacity, Fiegen not only serves as general contractor, but also works with the owner from the inception of a project. In the pre-construction phase, the company develops the design in association with an architect so that the practical applications of the project are addressed on the front end.

Fiegen Construction maintains a fleet of cranes for use on its projects plus a crane rental service.

In the construction management specialty, Fiegen takes on the management of the building phase of a project from beginning to end, supervising the bidding process and overseeing the construction. As a construction manager, the company works in conjunction with the owner and may utilize pre-selected subcontractors. "Owners are becoming more educated about the importance of professional construction management and design-build," says Fiegen. "It gives us all a chance to sit down and work out the details in advance. We call it 'value engineering' because the pre-planning can eliminate surprises and cost over-runs."

Fiegen Construction has been a leader in the area of construction equipment. In fact, it was the first company in South Dakota to use a pneumatic steel deck fastener system. "We are always willing to try something new to give more quality and greater economy to the client," says Fiegen.

Fiegen has been involved in the construction of some of the city's best known commercial and public facilities.

"We tested the pneumatic system in the field, then had it checked by experts. Now it's a specification standard."

Fiegen Construction also maintains a fleet of erection cranes and heavy rigging equipment, which are also rented or leased to other contractors.

ATTENTION TO QUALITY

Because doing a job the right way is important to the Fiegen family, weekly meetings are held at job sites to review progress. In addition, the Fiegens, father and sons, visit each job site several times weekly to keep a close eye on the work.

Having two layers of management overseeing a project can often prevent problems which may cause work delays and unnecessary expense. "When

In all of its projects, Fiegen Construction strives for innovation, quality control, and safety.

you're on a job site day in and day out like the job foreman, potential problems can sometimes go undetected," says Rusty Fiegen. "It helps when somebody else walks through who has a fresh eye and his mind on the complete project."

He adds that knowing the appropriate workers to assign to a project is also a key to success. "Our company is a manageable size so we know our people," he says. "We know their strengths and weaknesses and which jobs they are most suitable for."

As a satisfied client of Fiegen Construction, the Reverend James Andraschko of the Church of the Holy Spirit can attest to the company's outstanding work. "Their craftsmanship is superb, and they do not cut corners," he says. "They made absolutely sure that the project was done to our total satisfaction."

"Our company's greatest resource is its people," says Jeff Fiegen. "We have skilled craftsmen and operators who take pride in their work through continuous innovation, quality control, and safety. We're proud of our people and our reputation for quality, value engineering, and strict cost and schedule control."

Among the company's projects in Sioux Falls is the award-winning Church of the Holy Spirit.

I N JULY 1962, DR. KARL H. WEGNER, A LOCAL INTUITIVE physician who realized the lack of clinical pathology services in the Sioux Falls region, opened a two-employee laboratory in the basement of a local doctor's office. From those modest beginnings, the Laboratory of Clinical Medicine (LCM) has grown to become one of the most respected names in clinical testing in the upper Midwest. Today, the Sioux Falls

Through client service, LCM/Nichols Institute becomes an extension of the physician, clinic, and hospital laboratories.

facility serves approximately 200 hospitals in the region and performs specialized tests for patients nationwide.

LCM's reputation was enhanced in 1988 when it was acquired by Nichols Institute, an international diagnostic laboratory based in San Juan Capistrano, California. As a part of Nichols

What began as a two-employee laboratory is today an integral part of a comprehensive diagnostic network.

Institute's comprehensive diagnostic network, the Sioux Falls laboratory can now draw on the collective expertise of individual laboratories and academic associates nationwide. Nichols Institute regional laboratories such as LCM/ Sioux Falls make laboratory testing accessible and dependable on the local level. Nichols Institute operates 15 regional testing facilities in the United States and serves 28 international markets.

QUALITY TESTING CLOSE TO HOME

The LCM/Nichols Institute story began three decades ago with Dr. Wegner's vision to bring quality laboratory services to rural areas of South Dakota and neighboring states. Today, this revolutionary concept has become routine, as test samples from all over the region

and even the country arrive daily at the 32,000-square-foot laboratory facility in Sioux Falls.

During its early years, LCM/ Nichols Institute began sending consulting pathologists and medical technologists directly to small-town hospitals and clinics to support the laboratory's commitment to service, education, and research. In 1967, LCM/Nichols Institute brought on Dr. Durward M. Lang, who with his knowledge and experience in clinical testing instituted many improvements and new services, including the use of mobile Diagnostic Imaging testing units, which helped streamline patient care in outlying areas.

Under Dr. Lang's leadership, LCM/ Nichols Institute became one of the first laboratories in the Midwest to offer radioimmunoassay testing, a diagnostic technique using minute quantities of specimen. Dr. Lang also helped LCM/Nichols Institute establish the first mobile ultrasound program in the United States. The pioneering efforts of the founding pathologists significantly increased diagnostic efficiency and further ensured that quality medical care would be available in urban and rural areas.

DIAGNOSTIC SPECIALTIES

Today, virtually every type of diagnostic procedure, from the simplest blood work to complex nuclear tissue testing, is conducted by LCM/Nichols Institute's 21 staff pathologists and over 450 specially trained technologists, medical technicians, and support personnel. But over the years, the laboratory has developed some areas of specialization.

In the early 1980s, for example, LCM/Nichols Institute began offering a new blood test for allergies known as RAST. Since LCM joined Nichols in 1988, the Sioux Falls laboratory has handled all RAST testing for Nichols

Institute. With blood specimens arriving daily from hospitals and clinics nationwide, the LCM/Nichols Institute staff performs the tests on-site and reports the results within the same day to local physicians, thanks to modern instrumentation, state-of-the-art computer equipment, and remote printing capabilities.

Dr. Barry T. Pitt-Hart, who came to LCM/Nichols Institute in 1967, is medical director for South Dakota and has been instrumental in implementing much of the technology that has made LCM/Nichols Institute an industry leader in quality and service. For example, the remote printing capabilities that link the laboratory to physicians' offices, as well as thorough quality control programs, were put in place by Dr. Pitt-Hart.

For thousands of patients across the region and the country, Dr. Karl Wegner's vision has become a lifesaving resource. Nichols Institute has taken regional laboratories, like LCM, and consolidated them into one integrated, efficient laboratory system. Nichols Institute and LCM strive to maintain the standards of service and quality established by Dr. Wegner and others, while simultaneously developing new and better ways to meet the challenges of tomorrow. This commitment is guided by dedication to the community, to the medical staff, and to the patients LCM/Nichols Institute serves.

SOUTHEAST VOCATIONAL TECHNICAL INSTITUTE traces its history to 1968, when the State Board of Vocational Education appropriated $365,000 for the Sioux Falls School District to establish a local vo-tech school. That year, in a small addition on the north side of Lincoln High School, 118 students enrolled in classes ranging from practical nursing to diesel and airplane mechanics, industrial electronics, and data processing. Nearly 25 years later, Southeast Vocational Technical Institute is one of Sioux Falls' newest, most exciting landmarks. The school's impressive modern campus sharply contrasts the collection of older buildings scattered around the city that housed the Institute prior to 1990.

While students still register for courses in data processing, mechanics, and electronics, degree requirements have changed significantly to keep pace with expanding technology in those fields. Likewise, training in practical nursing has been replaced by more specialized courses in nuclear medicine, cardiovascular technology, and emergency medical technician training.

TOUCHING LIVES THROUGHOUT THE COMMUNITY

Today, Southeast Vocational Technical Institute's 980 career-minded students represent only a fraction of the people who benefit from its programs. "Last year, we touched 9,784 lives," says Terry Sullivan, Institute director since 1986. "From GED preparation to business and industry training at John Morrell & Co. and Hutchinson Technology to adult classes in cooking and the arts, people in this community rely on us to enhance the quality of their lives."

For example, the GED prep program helps adults without a high school diploma attain the General Equivalency Degree, often considered a ticket to higher learning and better employment opportunities. Likewise, the business and industry training division offers course work to local businesses to advance the skills of their workers. During the past three years, enrollment in Community Education Services (CES) classes has increased approximately 20 percent each year. CES offers about 100 continuing education classes each spring and fall, ranging from an introduction to computers to classes on estate planning, furniture upholstery, basic foreign language skills, and woodworking.

> "We're very conscious of being funded publicly by tax dollars," says Terry Sullivan, director. "We want to give back to South Dakota the services the citizens deserve."

But the major role of the Institute is in career training. Sophisticated, short-term career education is a popular alternative chosen by a rapidly growing segment of the population. With the workplace constantly changing and new opportunities opening up, it's not surprising that 60 percent of the students

Each year, more than 900 students take advantage of the Institute's focus on short-term education.

are 25 or older. The majority of those "non-traditional" students come from within a 50-mile radius of Sioux Falls, and graduates tend to stay in the city, as local growth creates exciting job opportunities. Currently, the Institute boasts an impressive 97 percent job placement rate, which the administration strives to maintain.

"We have regular department meetings to anticipate shifts in job needs," Sullivan says. "It only takes us six months to implement a new program of study, and we keep our finger on the pulse of the community to determine what kinds of skilled technicians are needed to ensure the economic vitality of the state."

MODERN COURSES AND FACILITIES

Southeast Vocational Technical Institute's variety of courses lead toward a two-year Associate of Applied Sciences degree. Always in tune with the needs of the local community, the school offers popular courses in nuclear medicine, cardiovascular and surgical technology, accounting, marketing, business administration, financial services, data processing, electronics, and CAD (computer-assisted design) technology. Because the Institute is accredited by the North Central Association of Colleges and Schools (the accrediting body for four-year colleges and universities in the region), students can transfer courses and credits to other post-secondary institutions.

Sixty full-time and numerous part-time faculty members, as well as 30 support and administrative personnel, deliver diverse programs and services at the Institute. The 56-acre campus is a showplace of vocational education, with its beautiful facilities and child care center. The Institute's sophisticated communications facilities include a satellite teleconferencing system that allows employers and students to participate in national and worldwide seminars. Plans are under way for a new Community Center, featuring a wellness center and additional facilities for new educational offerings.

According to Sullivan, it's all part of an ongoing commitment to meet state and community needs. "We're very conscious of being funded publicly by tax dollars," Sullivan says. "We want to give back to South Dakota the services the citizens deserve."

Christmas lights and tinsel cast a festive
glow over this downtown street scene in 1969.

McCrossan's Boys Ranch, a boarding
school and ranch for teenage boys just
north of town, has gained a reputation
for handling horses and instant recognition for the covered wagons it sends to
parades across the state.

SPIRIT OF SIOUX FALLS 1969 - 1992

1969
Eide Helmeke & Co.

1970
Sencore, Inc.

1971
EROS Data Center

1971
Howard Johnson Hotel

1972
Coldwell Banker GKR &
Associates

1972
Holiday Inn City Centre

1974
HY-VEE Food Stores, Inc.

1976
Minnegasco

1977
Kilian Community College

1977
Menumaster, Inc.

1977
Midland National Life
Insurance Company

1984
Prairie Tree Partners

1985
DAKOTACARE

1985
Sioux Falls Surgical Center

1988
Cellular One
of Sioux Falls

1988
Hutchinson
Technology, Inc.

1989
Charter Hospital
of Sioux Falls

1991
Huron University

EIDE HELMEKE & CO.

IDE HELMEKE & CO. HAS BEEN SUCCESSFUL IN serving clients in Sioux Falls since 1969. The local office is one of eight locations of Eide Helmeke & Co., which was founded 75 years ago in Fargo, North Dakota. In addition to the Sioux Falls and Fargo locations, the firm has offices in Aberdeen, South Dakota; Bismarck and Minot, North Dakota; Moorhead and Minneapolis, Minnesota; and

Phoenix, Arizona. With a total staff of over 200, Eide Helmeke & Co. offers vast expertise to the business community.

GENE'S STUDIO

Partner-in-charge Robert G. Wiedeman, CPA (left) and partner Kevin A. Doyle, CPA.

The Sioux Falls office is located in the new Commerce Center, a hub of riverfront development in Sioux Falls. Such a center of activity is an appropriate location for a firm which has advised and assisted many area companies on the road to success. Regarded as one of the city's outstanding accounting and tax firms, Eide Helmeke & Co. is equally well-known for its full range of consulting services.

"We cannot over-emphasize the importance of our clients' success," says Robert G. Wiedeman, CPA, partner-in-charge of the Sioux Falls office. "Our success directly depends on their success. That is our driving force to seek out better management methods, services, and products for our clients."

A FULL RANGE OF CLIENTS AND SERVICES

Eide Helmeke & Co. provides services to all types of businesses. "Our clients have provided us with an opportunity to develop a spectrum of services needed on a continuing basis for businesses to be successful," says Wiedeman. "Our services expand as the business grows. Sound planning in areas such as organizational structure and computer and financial accounting systems suited to the specific needs of the client is essential to the success of a business."

"An independent, objective analysis of a client's management system often reveals strengths and weaknesses the client may not notice," says Kevin A. Doyle, CPA, a partner in the Sioux Falls office. "We offer recommendations beyond traditional accounting and tax services. Our professionals provide services on the premise that we are a management resource to the client."

Adds Doyle, "In family-owned businesses, the need for succession planning becomes critical. Planning for the tax and cash flow consequences of buy-sell transactions is necessary in order to structure agreements to assure that the owner and business can continue to operate successfully. Our services address potential problems before they occur and help formulate solutions where ownership and management are changing."

QUALITY CLIENT SERVICE MAKES THE DIFFERENCE

"We incorporate the word 'innovative' into the definition of quality," says Wiedeman. "The technical aspects are, and always will be, the backbone of our services. In addition, we provide management ideas for our clients that enhance current and future operations.

"Employee benefit programs often contribute to employee job satisfaction and increased profits. Assisting management in establishing plans for employees is another specialty we have. Plans

> Regarded as one of the city's outstanding accounting and tax firms, Eide Helmeke & Co. is equally well-known for its full range of consulting services.

which benefit both employees and management can provide the competitive edge needed for a business to win."

Wiedeman continues, "We have a low staff turnover rate which provides continuity of service. Our people work together as a team to provide the client with quality services which help the client achieve success."

COMMITMENT TO GROWTH IN SIOUX FALLS

Wiedeman stresses the importance of the firm's participation in the community as a corporate citizen of Sioux Falls. "An integral part of our personnel development is their involvement in the community," he explains. "We have contributed money, time, and expertise to the Sioux Falls area's service, cultural, and religious organizations. We believe in the community. It is a privilege to be a part of the city's progress, and we intend to be a vital partner in its future.

"For over 20 years in Sioux Falls, we have approached each service provided as a means to contribute to the client's success. Their success assures us and the community a very bright future."

ADVANCED TECHNOLOGY HAS PLACED SOPHISTICATED electronics in homes and businesses the world over, ranging from VCRs to home theater to personal computers. When something goes wrong with one of these technological marvels, the average consumer must call a professional servicer, and that's where Sencore, Inc. enters the picture. ♦ The more than 250 people at this Sioux Falls-based

company work together to design, build, and sell innovative electronic test and measurement instruments used in servicing video, audio, cable, and computer equipment. According to Al Bowden, CEO of the second-generation family business, "Video service has become our backbone, but markets such as cable and computer service are exciting opportunity areas for our future expansion."

STAYING ABREAST OF CHANGING TECHNOLOGY

Sencore was founded in Chicago in 1951 by Al's father, Herb, and was relocated to Sioux Falls in 1970, at-

Sencore designs, builds, and sells innovative electronic test and measurement instruments used worldwide in servicing video, audio, cable, and computer equipment.

tracted by the area's superb quality of life. Today, Sencore is a fully integrated company, serving electronic service professionals worldwide. "We're not just a manufacturer," Bowden explains, "but more so an engineering and marketing firm that builds our own products."

Sencore's second generation, represented by co-owners Al and brother Doug Bowden, is committed to adapting to the technical challenges necessary to take Sencore into the 21st century. Sencore's highly trained employees continually design new equipment based on advances in the electronics industry. With each new product, the company deals with complex issues of marketability, design feasibility, and manufacturability, and brings these together in the shortest time possible.

"Because our markets are evolving so fast," Bowden says, "we work to shrink down our development time. There is often a very narrow window of opportunity for new products, so advance planning and execution are critical. We have shrunk this time down from four years to 18 months, but we must get better to stay competitive!"

CORPORATE STRATEGIES FOR THE FUTURE

Sencore's corporate strategies focus on quality, marketing, community service, and employee development. "In our quality effort, we're not satisfied with mere compliance to specifications," Bowden says. "We are striving for improvement on a continual basis. Our team accomplishes this by designing in excellent quality and constantly challenging our process."

Sencore's marketing strategy is grounded in selling directly to its customers. The company has found it can provide better quality support if the customer always talks to company headquarters in Sioux Falls. Sencore also services everything it sells, so customers come to count on the firm for answers long after a product is originally sold.

Community involvement is another part of the Sencore strategy. "We're proud of this community, and we want to be known as a leader in Sioux Falls,"

Bowden says. "We return more than 5 percent of our profits to our community. Being family owned locally in Sioux Falls is a real plus in that way."

Sencore's people are its greatest resource. The company is committed to employee training and development through a variety of efforts, including a degree completion program. Sencore employees are also partners in product teams, which draw members from every area of the company to design quality and value into a product from

In 1970, Sencore moved its headquarters to Sioux Falls to take advantage of the area's superb quality of life.

the beginning and help reduce development time. In the process, they cultivate a sense of ownership and pride for the product and the company.

Looking to the future, contract manufacturing is an important area for growth, as numerous firms have recognized Sencore's high quality capabilities and are relying on the firm to build their electronic-related products. "We are just starting to tap the potential in our outside manufacturing opportunities and are looking for great things to come from that market," says Bowden.

Likewise, Sencore's recent affiliation with AVS, a French electronics firm, promises further growth. This exciting partnership, spearheaded by brother Doug, will bring French technology in the area of broadcast and cable products to the United States and will allow Sencore to diversify into other markets, using its 40 years of video experience.

As technology continues to move ahead, Sencore is prepared to keep pace. Says Bowden, "We are a forward-looking engineering/manufacturing/marketing firm with an eye on a great future in Sioux Falls."

I N 1971, THE SIOUX FALLS ARENA WAS CELEBRATING ITS first anniversary as a new civic attraction, and the Sioux Falls airport, through an expansion, was enjoying its new status as a regional facility. On March 1 of that year, these two facilities were complemented by the opening of a hotel convenient to both, the 200-room Howard Johnson Hotel. Located on West Russell Street, the hotel's proximity to Interstates 29 and 90 makes it convenient for motorists as well.

One of the first convention hotels in Sioux Falls, the Howard Johnson has been, for more than 20 years, a popular site for both large and small meetings and a favorite lodging facility for business and leisure travelers. The hotel was built and developed by former Sioux Falls resident Sherwood L. Corner, a Washington High School graduate and the father of the hotel's current general manager, Mark Corner. Sherwood Corner's company, Vernwood Developers, Inc., also operates the Howard Johnson Hotel in Rapid City, South Dakota; a HoJo Inn in Billings, Montana; and the Brimark Inn, which is adjacent to the Howard Johnson in Sioux Falls. In all, Vernwood Developers boasts approximately 750 rooms across the Northern Plains.

OUTSTANDING CONVENTION FACILITIES

Easy to find and easy to get to, the Howard Johnson Hotel in Sioux Falls has 26,000 square feet of meeting space that can easily and efficiently accommodate groups as large as 1,500. The convention facilities include nine meeting rooms and a spacious exhibit foyer, all located on the main floor for the convenience of guests. No structural poles or columns obstruct the view in the large meeting rooms, and teleconferencing capabilities are available to meet the most exacting modern specifications. The hotel staff includes professional meeting planners who are available to make arrangements for any size meeting.

Excellent food service can also be expected by convention guests at the Howard Johnson. "We're very proud of

Located on West Russell Street, the 200-room Howard Johnson Hotel offers excellent service, outstanding food, attractive guest rooms, and versatile meeting facilities.

our food and beverage staff," says Mark Corner, who has been on the hotel staff for 16 years. "We've been told by convention and travel planners that our food quality is the best in the state of South Dakota. That's why so many groups come back to us again and again."

From an outstanding variety of menu selections, the hotel's catering staff can plan a special dining experience for large banquets or small private parties, and for buffet or plate service. The hotel's competent, experienced chefs and servers always execute the plans with both professionalism and originality.

The Howard Johnson Hotel hosts approximately five conventions and meetings each week, for a total of about 250 events annually. That accounts for a large percentage of the conventions booked each year in Sioux Falls. Offering 110 additional guest rooms, the Brimark Inn, located just 50 feet from the front desk of the Howard Johnson, can be utilized to help accommodate larger conventions. Together the two facilities, both managed by Corner, offer the largest concentration of hotel rooms at a single location in Sioux Falls and one of the largest convention facilities in the state of South Dakota.

DRAWING BUSINESS AND LEISURE TRAVELERS

As impressive as the hotel's convention activity may be, that segment accounts for only a third of the annual business at the Howard Johnson Hotel. The other two-thirds is generated in equal parts by individual business travelers and leisure guests.

Corner says that for the business traveler, the Howard Johnson Executive Section is a special lure and an attractive perk. Privileges include complimentary morning coffee and paper, a complimentary welcome snack upon arrival, facsimile and copying services, and VIP pre-registration status. "The Executive Section is our way of thanking our regular business guests," adds Corner.

Leisure travelers will find 200 of the most attractive hotel rooms in the state, each featuring elegant color schemes, solid oak furniture, brass and ceramic decorative features, and double vanities. Guests can relax or exercise at the hotel's indoor-outdoor pool or unwind in the jacuzzi or saunas.

Other amenities include a restaurant that offers outstanding food prepared and served by the hotel's food service staff, as well as a night spot that features live entertainment. The Oaks

Restaurant, open from 6 a.m. to 10 p.m. daily, serves up an extensive menu, including steaks, seafood, chicken, and Italian dishes, along with a complete salad bar. The newly expanded and redecorated Sunbird Lounge, which seats 275 people, is one of the city's most popular gathering places. Live entertainment Monday through Saturday evenings, a huge dance floor, a daily "$1 Dinner Buffet," and video lottery machines make the Sunbird Lounge the place to be in Sioux Falls for fun.

Economy-minded travelers enjoy staying at the nearby Brimark Inn, a "luxury for less" hotel built in 1976, five years after the Howard Johnson was opened. The extras offered at the Brimark Inn include a free continental breakfast, a large outdoor heated pool, and color satellite television.

A FORMULA FOR SUCCESS

The excellent service, outstanding food, attractive guest rooms, and versatile meeting facilities at both locations bring old customers back and new customers in—a formula for success in the hotel business and in Sioux Falls.

"With Sioux Falls' continued bright economic outlook," says Corner, "we are looking forward to expanding our meeting and banquet rooms to accommodate groups of up to 2,000 people. We're also making plans to add a wing of 15 luxury suites to the Howard Johnson Hotel."

Growing with Sioux Falls and planning for the future, the management and staff at the Howard Johnson Hotel and its sister facility, the Brimark Inn, are taking steps to further enhance a well-earned reputation for excellence throughout South Dakota.

Top: The hotel's experienced food service staff caters meals for virtually any size meeting or convention. Bottom: Together, the Howard Johnson and the nearby Brimark Inn offer the largest concentration of hotel rooms at a single location in Sioux Falls.

SINCE ITS FOUNDING IN 1971, THE EARTH RESOURCES Observation Systems (EROS) Data Center has been Sioux Falls' window on the world. Space-age photographs of recent global events—such as the Kuwait oil well fires or the eruption of Mt. Pinatubo—were transmitted via satellite directly to this federal facility in Sioux Falls. ◆ The EROS Data Center (EDC) is a research field center

of the U.S. Geological Survey's National Mapping Division. It was established more than two decades ago to receive, process, and distribute data from NASA Landsat satellites. "Our early mission was to give the scientific

with another 9 million aerial photographs. The EDC is also a clearinghouse for data collected by foreign Landsat ground reception stations and Earth-observing satellites deployed by other countries.

Center has contributed to the war against drugs by providing satellite images of illegal vegetation in areas of South America as part of the U.S. counter-narcotics program. Since 1984, the EDC has offered technical support in the development of a famine warning system to serve participating countries in the Sahel region of Africa.

SERVING THE WORLD SCIENTIFIC COMMUNITY

Because of its location in Sioux Falls— roughly the center of the continental United States—the EDC is uniquely able to receive "real-time" electronic signals from Earth-orbiting satellites. The signals are used for developing comprehensive data sets of most of the North American continent or other large land masses.

In support of the Center's mission, one of the largest computer complexes in the Department of the Interior is housed at the Sioux Falls facility. Over 100 federal, state, and commercial offices are also linked to the Center for data inquiries. Each year, the EDC distributes approximately 250,000 data products in response to more than 60,000 inquiries from scientists and resource managers around the world.

The EDC is also a major participant in the U.S. Global Change Research Program, which studies such phenomena as global warming. Data from the Center provided to scientists worldwide improves their understanding of the planet and their ability to predict global change.

As a key player in NASA's "Mission to Planet Earth," the Center plans to process and archive land-related data from NASA satellites and the manned space station in the late-1990s. In preparation for that mission, plans are currently being made for a major expansion of the Sioux Falls facility to accommodate increased data storage and scientific staffing required for the NASA program.

"We're excited about our role in this vital project," Lauer says. "The growth of the EROS Data Center in response to this critical new look at our planet will continue a tradition of service to the world scientific community well beyond the year 2000."

The facility's reception area welcomes visitors to Sioux Falls' window on the world.

community a new perspective on the Earth," explains Donald T. Lauer, the Center's acting chief. "Since then, our job has grown, technology has improved, and the applications of the data we collect have grown."

Today, the EDC holds the world's largest collection of Earth images and photographs acquired by aircraft and satellites. In fact, 3 million satellite images are stored at the Center, along

This vast body of information is put to use in a variety of ways. Since its inception, the Center has provided land-surface data to national and international organizations involved in land management and environmental assessment activities, from studying desert temperature changes to monitoring vegetation patterns of the Nile Delta.

Recently, the EDC responded to requests from the Department of Defense and U.S. intelligence agencies by supplying digitally processed and enhanced satellite images in support of Operation Desert Storm. Likewise, the

The EROS Data Center in Sioux Falls is a research field center of the U.S. Geological Survey's National Mapping Division.

The Center also uses information from French, Japanese, and other foreign satellite systems to produce high quality image maps for a variety of scientific uses, from weather system analysis to land management programs.

APPLYING DATA TO EARTH SCIENCE PROBLEMS

Working closely with NASA, the National Oceanic and Atmospheric Administration (NOAA), various Department of Interior organizations, and other federal agencies, the EDC helps to develop advanced systems and techniques for applying Earth observations and other geographic information to Earth science problems. "Basically, we're in the business of discovering how best to use the vast array of information these satellites are sending us," Lauer says. "We want to ensure the best use of the millions of pieces of information stored at the EROS Data Center."

Part of this mission involves studies designed to improve the world's understanding of the mechanisms and processes leading to global environmental change. To support this research, the Center combines a multi-disciplinary scientific staff in geology, hydrology, cartography, geography, agronomy, soils science, forestry, meteorology, and climatology with engineering expertise in systems development, telecommunications, and computer science.

"We are a state-of-the-art facility," Lauer says. "But we're also responsible for continuing the development of what 'state-of-the-art' actually means."

The information stored in the archives of the EROS Data Center is made available to researchers and scientists through the Federal Land Remote Sensing Research Program. This program allows federal agencies, universities, and other organizations to assign scientists and researchers to the Center on a full-time basis with complete access to its comprehensive analytical equipment, data, and research facilities.

"As the need to increase the world's understanding of the planet grows, so will the mission of the EROS Data Center," says Lauer.

Images and information from every corner of the globe will continue to pour into this Sioux Falls-based facility, helping man keep a clear eye on Planet Earth.

This mosaic was created by the EROS Data Center with 15 satellite images gathered by Advanced Very High Resolution Radiometer sensors on two NOAA satellites.

LONG BEFORE CONSTRUCTION BEGAN IN 1967 ON THE Holiday Inn City Centre, Fort Dakota occupied the site in what was then known as the "gateway to the West." In fact, the first photograph ever made in Sioux Falls shows a group of settlers posing in front of the fort, built in 1865 as a shelter amid the frequent Indian wars. Ever since, the two-block area surrounding this historic corner has been a center for hospitality in Sioux Falls.

In 1871, the Cataract Hotel, the city's first hotel, was erected on the site. Over a century later, the Holiday Inn City Centre continues the tradition of hospitality and dedication to guest comfort that were the hallmarks of the old hotel. Richard Nixon, George Bush, Cloris Leachman, Jack Benny, Arnold Schwartzenegger, and Elvis Presley, as well as countless business travelers, entertainers, and tourists, have all made the hotel, at the heart of the city, their Sioux Falls address.

CATERING TO BUSINESS AND LEISURE TRAVELERS

The Holiday Inn City Centre is the only hotel in Sioux Falls offering a concierge service to provide information and answer guest questions about the hotel's array of services. Over 300 recently remodeled guest rooms, including king sofa rooms and an executive level, feature all the amenities expected in a modern hotel: color cable television, AM/FM radios, a message waiting feature, rooms for non-smokers and handicapped guests, valet services, complimentary airport limousine, and free overnight parking in the adjacent bi-level parking garage. The Holiday Inn City Centre offers additional amenities to its guests, such as complimentary morning coffee and newspaper and express check-out.

The convenient downtown location—close to unique shops, some of the city's best restaurants, and numerous corporate headquarters—makes the Holiday Inn City Centre a logical choice for most VIP and business travelers. But the hotel's recreation and leisure offerings attract many guests who come just for the fun of it. The hotel's Holidome offers a complete

Top: Over 300 recently remodeled guest rooms feature all the amenities expected in a modern hotel.
Bottom: Burgundy's Rooftop Restaurant offers fine dining accompanied by a panoramic view of Sioux Falls.

indoor recreation center, with indoor/outdoor pool, whirlpool and sauna, exercise equipment, ping-pong and pool tables, a putting green, and an electronic game room. Guests also enjoy discounts at local health club facilities. Honeymoon and weekend packages are available for special occasions.

> Richard Nixon, George Bush, Cloris Leachman, Jack Benny, Arnold Schwartzenegger, and Elvis Presley, as well as countless business travelers, entertainers, and tourists, have all made the hotel their Sioux Falls address.

For great family dining or a romantic dinner for two, guests never have to leave the hotel. Burgundy's Rooftop Restaurant, offering a panoramic view of Sioux Falls, is truly one of the city's fine restaurants. The Country Kettle, open daily from 6 a.m. to 10 p.m., is known for its great deli lunches and sumptuous dinner specials. With 220 seats, the Country Kettle is one of the largest restaurants in Sioux Falls. The King George Pub and Terrace, the official center of the city's annual St. Patrick's Day celebration, is open seven days a week for casual relaxation and enjoyment.

The Holiday Inn City Centre is a frequent host for local meetings and special events, which are customized and presented in the elegant Starlite Ballroom, with its shimmering chandeliers, or the spacious International Rooms, with flexible floor plans for any size gathering. Additional meeting facilities are utilized throughout the year by business, fraternal, and service groups. Dedicated to making every meeting or event successful, the City Centre staff provides many extra touches, whether catering an elegant banquet or setting up audio-visual facilities for a business gathering. Weddings, political rallies and victory parties, family and class reunions, and special events of every type are also celebrated at the Holiday Inn City Centre.

TWO DECADES OF SERVICE

On the heels of its first 20 years of service, the Holiday Inn City Centre is proud of its well-earned position in the Sioux Falls community and of the city's 1992 designation by *Money* magazine as "America's Best Place to Live." By maintaining the superior level of courteous service local residents and travelers have come to expect, the hotel hopes to further contribute to the community's growing national reputation.

As it enters a third decade as the city's premier hotel, the Holiday Inn City Centre, its management, and staff are committed to perpetuating a long-time tradition of hospitality in the heart of Sioux Falls.

IN 1972, WHEN EARL GERLACH, LeROY KRUSE, AND DON Randolph formed GKR Realty, houses in the Tuthill area of Sioux Falls were selling for $35,000. Today, those same properties are garnering up to $160,000 each. After weathering two decades of inflation and change in the real estate industry, Coldwell Banker GKR & Associates continues to help families find the perfect home. And in the process, the

firm has become one of Sioux Falls' most successful real estate partnerships.

"When I started selling real estate," remembers LeRoy Kruse, president of the firm, "we sold a lot of homes for around $23,000. Twenty years later, they are going for $58,000 to $60,000. And still, real estate in Sioux Falls is one of the best values in the country."

According to the Multiple Listing Service of Sioux Falls, the median sale price in 1992 for a home was up approximately $5,000 from the previous year—definitely a good sign, says Kruse. "Real estate is still a growth market in Sioux Falls," he explains. "Locally, our industry didn't experience a recession in the late '80s and early '90s like a lot of other areas did. That's a sign that our city has a solid economy and that the real estate industry in Sioux Falls is working hard for our buyers and sellers."

Oftentimes, a home listed by Coldwell Banker GKR & Associates doesn't even make it on the market before it is sold. In fact, the firm sells homes faster on average than its local and national counterparts according to the number of days a property is on the market.

TWO DECADES OF GROWTH

Today, over 30 agents work with Coldwell Banker GKR & Associates, including founders Gerlach and Kruse. Since 1989, the firm has been a member of the Sears Financial Network, which encompasses over 1,400 real estate offices nationwide. In 1991, the Sioux Falls firm was ranked 79th among those members—something Kruse is understandably proud of.

"We're not a large firm compared to some other Coldwell Banker offices," he says, "but we work hard. We average one transaction every 12 hours and list

over 500 homes each year. Our agents have more than 350 years of combined real estate experience. We know Sioux Falls, and we know real estate."

Currently, about 97 percent of the firm's total sales are in the residential market, while just 3 percent come from agricultural or investment property. Within its residential expertise, Coldwell Banker GKR & Associates sells homes in every price range. "We recently sold a home for $40,000," Kruse says, "and then turned around and sold another for $600,000. There is a wide range of home prices in Sioux Falls, with a great deal of activity on the upper end. But virtually every family can still find a home they can afford, regardless of their price range."

Kruse adds that the biggest change in real estate sales over the years has been in the area of financing. "When we started, there were five basic types of home financing," he remembers. "Today, there are 50. As a result, real estate lenders must be more involved with each buyer and seller. It's good in that it gives the buyer more options, but it makes real estate a lot more complicated than it once was."

Likewise, Realtors® today do more pre-qualifying and spend more time with buyers and sellers working to make each transaction go smoothly. "With interest rates fluctuating and the market shifting, changes in real estate happen more quickly," says Kruse. "But the public is more knowledgeable than before, and that's a better situation for the Realtor®. Potential buyers have usually done some planning before they start looking at houses. They know about what their price range is and the

LeRoy Kruse, current president, helped found GKR Realty in 1972.

part of town and kind of house they want. That helps us help them."

And that's one thing that definitely hasn't changed in 20 years. Coldwell Banker GKR & Associates is still in the business of helping families find the perfect home.

Over 30 agents work from the firm's headquarters at 1000 East 41st Street in Sioux Falls.

WHEN HY-VEE FOOD STORES CAME TO SIOUX FALLS in 1974 to open a store at 26th Street and Sycamore, the company was following a pattern of growth started in 1938. That year, Charles L. Hyde and David M. Vredenburg, along with a baker's dozen other investors, incorporated their small grocery chain in Lamoni, Iowa. ◆ The two men had been partners in the grocery

Today's Hy-Vee includes all the elements that make a complete shopping experience for the busy modern family: bakeries, delicatessens, pharmacies, and specialty sections.

business in a handful of Iowa farming communities since 1930. Their personalities complemented each other, and their dedication to service—some of the original groceries were called "Service Stores"—helped the business grow. The company continued to expand throughout Iowa and the Midwest. In 1953, all stores were renamed Hy-Vee in honor of founders Hyde and Vredenburg—a name chosen in a companywide contest soliciting ideas from employees. The company itself, then known as Hyde & Vredenburg, did not officially become Hy-Vee Food Stores, Inc. until 1963.

GROWING WITH THE COMMUNITY

Hy-Vee's growth in Sioux Falls has been rapid, much like the growth of the city itself. After opening its first local store in 1974 on the corner of 26th and

Sycamore, the company built a new store in 1977 at the busy corner of Louise and 41st Street. The nearby Empire Mall shopping center, which draws 10 million shoppers each year, has contributed significantly to the store's high profile. From 1984 to 1991, Hy-Vee acquired the former Safeway store at 33rd Street and Minnesota Avenue and replaced its two original locations with new stores.

"Our newest locations are 60,000-square-foot stores," says Jim Hootman, director for the 49th and Louise location. "That's about 2 1/2 times larger than our original Sioux Falls store. All three have the diversity for one-stop shopping."

Today's Hy-Vee includes all the elements that make a complete shopping experience for the busy modern family. The three Sioux Falls stores have their own bakeries, delicatessens, and pharmacies, as well as specialty sections that make them unique. The two newest locations even house convenient branches of Marquette Bank. "In addition to our floral shops, pharma-

cies, and delis," says Hootman, "we've got fresh seafood shops, meat and cheese islands, fresh pizza shops, salad and juice bars, video rental departments, and even a baseball card shop in our two new stores. We try to do it all."

A MAJOR EMPLOYER IN SIOUX FALLS

With over 800 employees and an annual local payroll of $5.5 million, Hy-Vee is one of the largest employers in Sioux Falls. According to Hootman, being a part of the Hy-Vee family is a great experience. "We're an employee-owned company," he explains. "Up to 25 percent of our net profit is paid into a profit sharing plan at no cost to our employees. We also have an in-store monthly bonus plan for regular and full-time employees."

The company also believes in letting its work force do their jobs according to the realities of the local market. In Sioux Falls that commitment played an important part in the design and creation of the two newest Hy-Vee stores. "Company officials brought the plans to Sioux Falls and basically asked us, 'What do you think?'" Hootman recalls. "As a result, we have the only two stores in the entire company with seafood shops that have the East Coast look. Our managers have the latitude to mold each store to the needs of their customers and the individual market."

Some other features of Hy-Vee stores include wider aisles in the new stores, more user-friendly shelving, and a sense of environmental responsibility. "We give a five cent refund for bags returned and reused for a customer's order," Hootman says. "We also use dishes instead of paper plates in our 49th Street deli department. It's just one more way to show our commitment to the environment."

Hootman says that's only because the company is looking ahead to Sioux Falls' future. "These stores prove our commitment to the growth of this city," he adds. "Modern grocery stores must be combination food and drug centers, open 24 hours a day for everyone's convenience. Through diversity and service, we want to be the store of the '90s in Sioux Falls."

SIOUX FALLS WAS STILL A SMALL PRAIRIE VILLAGE when J.H. Miller Jr. established his local gas distribution business on March 31, 1883. With a 99-year franchise from the village government, Miller opened a plant at 10th Street and Second Avenue to distribute manufactured gas, a chemically produced lighting and heating source commonly used before the commercial transport of

natural gas via pipelines was possible. By 1886, Miller's original plant had failed, and the newly established Sioux Falls Gas Company began service to fill the community's growing energy demands.

It wasn't until 1931 that the distribution of natural gas—the clean, inexpensive energy source used in so many area homes today—was first begun in Sioux Falls. In 1940, locally based Central Electric and Telephone purchased the company and operated it for over 30 years. Minnesota Gas Company, now known as Minnegasco, acquired the local natural gas properties in 1976.

Headquartered in Minneapolis, Minnegasco today continues the long-time heritage of service that residents have come to expect since 1883. The company currently meets the natural gas needs of more than 670,000 residential and business customers in 236 Minnesota, Nebraska, and South Dakota communities. As a division of Arkla, Inc., one of the largest natural gas companies in the United States, Minnegasco ties into a pipeline system with tremendous reserves. In fact, Arkla, Inc. operates over 14,000 miles of pipeline handling more than 1 trillion cubic feet of natural gas each year.

Employing more than 1,700 people in the three-state area, Minnegasco maintains 39,000 service lines and 600 miles of mains in South Dakota alone. All are maintained and upgraded regularly to ensure safe, reliable service to the company's customers. In South Dakota, Minnegasco serves over 44,000 commercial and residential customers primarily in the southeastern part of the state from its headquarters in Sioux Falls.

AN INDUSTRY LEADER

A leader in industry innovation, Minnegasco was the first gas distribution company in the United States to begin large-scale installation of the Accu-Read® System. Pioneered by Minnegasco, the system uses radio frequency technology to read customers' meters.

> Employing more than 1,700 people in the three-state area, Minnegasco maintains 39,000 service lines and 600 miles of mains in South Dakota alone.

By simply driving a specially equipped van through metered areas, the AccuRead System can read up to 24,000 meters in a single workday. Sioux Falls was the first city on Minnegasco's system to be equipped for remote meter reading.

Meeting the natural gas demands of a geographic region with four distinct climates requires innovation in planning and a commitment to develop state-of-the-art facilities. To that end, Minnegasco maintains underground storage, liquefied natural gas storage, and propane storage facilities to ensure continuous access to cost-effective energy, even on the coldest winter days when demands exceed available pipeline supplies.

Beyond bringing an affordable energy source to South Dakota's businesses and residents, Minnegasco works hard to be a good corporate citizen. In 1991, the company paid $1.9 million in sales taxes and another $685,000 in property taxes.

The company's Community Involvement Programs encourage employees to volunteer their time and talents to the communities in which they live. In Sioux Falls, Minnegasco employees de-

liver Meals on Wheels to shut-in and elderly citizens. They also participate in the March of Dimes Walk America, Toys for Tots Fund Drive, and Junior Achievement's classroom programs.

Each year, Minnegasco makes charitable contributions in the areas of human services, education, the arts, and community development. For example, the company earmarks two-thirds of its human services budget for the United Way in 50 towns and cities in the three-state service area. Employees and retirees contribute an additional $118,000 to those local agencies through individual donations. In 1991, approximately 200 Minnegasco employees and retirees donated nearly $9,000 to educational institutions in South Dakota, Minnesota, and Nebraska. The company matched those gifts dollar-for-dollar, bringing the total contribution to area colleges and universities to over $17,000.

In partnership with the Salvation Army, Minnegasco also offers the Heat-Share program, which assists customers who cannot pay their winter heating bills and helps implement energy-conservation measures.

In 1992, 15 Minnegasco employees helped plan, organize, set up checkpoints, and cook and serve 800 hotdogs for Walk America, a fundraising event for the March of Dimes.

Over the years, Sioux Falls has come to depend on natural gas for a variety of energy uses, and Minnegasco has met that growing need since 1976. As Sioux Falls races toward a new century, Minnegasco is taking steps to ensure that the supply of clean, efficient natural gas will always be a part of the city's exciting future.

FOR MILLIONS OF CONSUMERS, THE MICROWAVE OVEN has become an indispensable household appliance. Although the first microwave ovens were produced at the end of World War II, the popularity of the appliance did not become widespread until the early 1970s, when technology was improved and new standards for the ovens were set by the federal government. ◆ In 1971, annual sales surpassed 100,000 units, and since then, the American public has not stopped clamoring for this timesaving appliance. Since 1977—relatively early in the history of the modern microwave oven—Sioux Falls has been a manufacturing center for microwave ovens in the United States, thanks to the presence of Litton Industries. Based in Beverly Hills, California, Litton today operates Menumaster, Inc., a wholly-owned subsidiary located in Sioux Falls and a world leader in the manufacture and marketing of commercial microwave ovens.

REFINING THE TECHNOLOGY

The discovery that high frequency radio waves, such as those generated by a magnetron or vacuum tube, could cook food was made shortly after World War II. It was determined that radio waves, when confined in a metal cavity or oven, could vibrate water molecules within food and that the resulting molecular friction, or heat, cooked the food. The first commercial ovens were introduced in 1947 for reheating and reconstituting foods in restaurants and institutions. These primitive microwave ovens were large, freestanding units that were unreliable, inefficient, and expensive.

In 1953, Charles "Tex" Thornton left Hughes Aircraft to purchase Litton Industries of California. A small electronics firm then based in San Carlos, Litton was primarily involved in the production of electron tubes for military-related radar applications. But Thornton was interested in developing a consumer-oriented line of products, and in 1954 stated publicly that the recently purchased company, renamed Litton Industries, would someday be in the cooking business.

The San Carlos plant, home of the Electron Tube Division of Litton, was headed by a creative physicist named Dr. Norman Moore, who had been with the company and its predecessor since 1948. Dr. Moore was interested in developing and refining the "cooking tube," which had been pioneered by the Raytheon Company for use in its microwave Radarange™ ovens.

In 1963, Dr. Moore convinced Tex Thornton to allow him to split off a team of 20 employees from the division to explore microwave applications. With Thornton's support, Moore set up a laboratory and production facility in Atherton, California, and the new plant began refining and improving microwave cooking technology. His efforts eventually helped develop an oven product that was feasible and profitable to manufacture, and the plant soon began producing ovens for the consumer market with great success.

MAKING MICROWAVE OVENS IN SIOUX FALLS

In 1977, Litton Industries built a manufacturing facility in Sioux Falls for the production of consumer ovens, including the "Meal-In-One" large-capacity ovens, the Micro-Browner, and the Generation II line of microwaves. The facility continued to manufacture consumer ovens for a number of years. But in 1989, Litton recognized an opportunity to establish itself more firmly in the

Menumaster manufactures an assortment of microwave ovens for commercial use, including the Jet-Wave™ (above), a combination microwave/convection large-capacity oven.

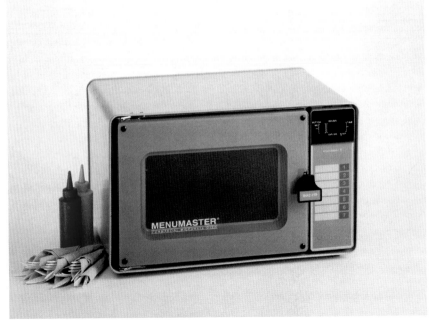

food service market and converted its operations to the manufacture of microwave ovens for commercial use.

Today, Sioux Falls is the corporate headquarters and distribution center of Menumaster, which also maintains branch offices in Toronto, London, and Sidney. In 1992, the Sioux Falls operation moved to a new 85,000-square-foot facility at 700 East 54th Street in the Sioux Empire Development Park. Currently, Menumaster's 180 local employees manufacture seven commercial oven models, from compact to large-capacity sizes, for use in hospitals and other institutions, hotels, restaurants, and snack bars.

A LEADER IN COMMERCIAL OVEN TECHNOLOGY

Many innovations and new features have been developed for commercial ovens by Litton and Menumaster to make food preparation more efficient and convenient for customers in the food service industry. For example, the companies pioneered the variable power oven control, TimeSaver™ combination push buttons and dial timers,

Many innovations and new features have been developed for commercial ovens by Litton and Menumaster to make food preparation more efficient and convenient for customers in the food service industry.

solid state timers, the MicroPopper,™ and large-capacity ovens for cooking in bulk and for reheating and defrosting. Menumaster also created the Jet-Wave,™ which is a combination microwave/convection large-capacity oven.

Other Menumaster oven features include Electronic Vari-Power,™ which provides a choice of five power levels at the touch of a button; Defrost II,® which thaws foods faster than conventional microwave defrost systems; and "Two-stage cooking," which combines defrosting and heating functions in one setting. In addition, Menumaster's "rotating stirrer system" distributes microwaves in an even, uniform pattern for quick, efficient heating.

Several unique oven features have been developed specifically for the restaurant industry. The "self diagnostic" feature verifies correct operation of the electronic timer to assure uniformity of food preparation. The Menumaster "cook cycle count" keeps track of specific menu items and quantities of each prepared daily to help restauranteurs determine the popularity of those foods. A "message scrolling function" allows a customized message to be displayed on the oven, and the "change time" feature allows any time and power setting to be entered with touch-button ease and without affecting existing programs.

As an inheritor of the technological advances made by Dr. Moore and his team just three decades ago, Menumaster has made enormous strides in recent years that have sent its products to the top of today's commercial microwave oven industry. With a comprehensive product line designed to meet the changing needs of the industry, Menumaster continues to lead the field in the service, marketing, and manufacture of commercial microwave ovens in Sioux Falls.

O NE OF THE TOP INSURANCE COMPANIES IN THE country, Midland National Life Insurance Company has enjoyed steady growth, stability of leadership, and industry success over the course of its 86-year history. From its home base in Sioux Falls, Midland today operates in 49 states, the District of Columbia, and Puerto Rico. The company employs 360 people in Sioux Falls and works with

more than 17,000 licensed sales professionals throughout the United States.

WATERTOWN BEGINNINGS

In 1906, Frank L. Bramble and a secretary opened the first office of the Dakota Mutual Life Insurance Company on the historic Granite Block of

Midland National Life has provided distinguished service since its founding in 1906.

Watertown, South Dakota, about 100 miles north of Sioux Falls. The company was a venture conceived by Bramble and partners D.M. Banister, W.B. Cannon, Dr. H.M. Finnerud, John B. Hanten, and John W. Martin.

The company grew slowly and steadily during the early years, even as it

faced the economic challenges of World War I, the Great Depression, the Dust Bowl, and World War II. In 1925, the company took the name under which it still operates today, Midland National Life Insurance Company. Reflecting its growth, the firm in 1950 moved into a new building on Maple Street in downtown Watertown.

In 1961, William A. Rigsbee became president of Midland, a position which he still holds today. Under his strong and dynamic leadership, the company has achieved an annual growth rate of 15 percent. During Rigsbee's tenure, Midland National Life Insurance Company also has increased life insurance in force from $275 million to $50 billion, assets from $29 million to $1.5 billion, and annual revenue (premium and investment income) from $6 million to more than $400 million.

Midland expanded its operations in 1968 with the acquisition of North American Management, Inc., a broker-dealer specializing in the distribution of mutual funds, and Investors Life Insurance Company of Nebraska, which has been developed into a special marketing outlet for Midland.

A major corporate change was made in 1977 with the relocation of company headquarters from Watertown to Sioux Falls. The present home office, the distinctive "gold" building, was designed to mirror part of the downtown Sioux Falls skyline. The Sioux Falls staff directs operations for Midland, as well as Investors Life Insurance Company.

CORPORATE OBJECTIVES AND SUCCESS

Two major corporate objectives guide operations at Midland National Life Insurance Company. One is to be a low-cost provider of life insurance and annuity products, which requires the

company to keep administrative costs down. The second is to remain a leader in developing new and innovative products that meet consumer needs in the ever-changing industry and economic environments.

The company's success in meeting these objectives, plus careful underwriting, ample surplus, and prudent investments, is reflected in Midland's position and ratings in the insurance industry. Of the 1,800 life insurance companies in the United States, Midland ranks in the top 30, based on new paid sales volume, which is in excess of

William A. Rigsbee, Midland's president and chairman, has been with the company since 1961.

$12 billion. A.M. Best, the nation's leading independent appraiser of life insurance companies, gives Midland an A+ Superior rating, the highest offered. Standard & Poor's has assigned Midland an AA+ (Excellent) rating based on the company's capital adequacy, solid liquidity, financial flexibility, and outstanding position in the nation's life insurance industry. Midland also was recently named one of the top 11 life insurance companies in America by *USA Today* based on the Weiss Research index of financial strength.

From its beginnings in Watertown at the turn of the century to the company's gleaming present in its landmark Sioux Falls headquarters building, Midland National Life Insurance Company has matured into a national leader in the insurance industry.

KILIAN COMMUNITY COLLEGE HAS BEEN PROVIDING career-oriented education for adults since its founding in 1977 as the North Central University Center. It was formed by Augustana College, Sioux Falls College, and the North American Baptist Seminary to provide college credit to adults. ♦ The college was renamed in 1985 to honor its founding president, Thomas Kilian. At that time, it began

offering its first degrees as a private, nonprofit, two-year college. Kilian's board of directors is composed of community leaders who volunteer their time to the college.

Accredited by the North Central Association of Colleges and Schools, Kilian serves the Sioux Falls region as a "college without walls," utilizing classrooms provided by its founding institutions and businesses throughout Sioux Falls. A capital fund drive was recently approved for Kilian by the Community Appeals Committee of the Sioux Falls Area Chamber of Commerce. Scheduled to begin March 1, 1993 and end July 31, 1993, the program's projected $600,000 in proceeds will be used by the college to acquire classroom space and administrative offices. For the past 15 years, Kilian has rented space from Sioux Falls College, but changing needs at both institutions compel a move to be completed by June of 1994.

CAREER-ORIENTED EDUCATION

"Hands-on" learning is the creed of the first college in South Dakota founded to meet the educational needs of adults. Kilian's faculty is composed of specialists with extensive work experience who teach their professions. Individual attention is a vital part of the Kilian approach.

Instructors refrain from the boring lecture style often associated with college courses, favoring problem-solving class projects. Consequently, students gain from the close interaction between instructors and classmates anxious to consider and examine the application of class material.

Students enrolled in the fire science program at Kilian Community College are familiar with class interruptions. If

the fire alarm sounds, the students and the instructor (all on-duty fire fighters) leave the classroom (the fire station) to answer the call. As one instructor describes it, "We practice what we teach!"

Students at Kilian are a highly motivated group. With a median age of 33, many are pursuing crucial career

Both students and instructors in Kilian's fire science program serve as on-duty fire fighters and hold class in the fire station.

education for the first time. "For numerous students, Kilian is their initial educational accomplishment," says Ron MacDonald, Kilian's president. "Frequently, it is also their first chance to achieve a goal they originally thought beyond their reach."

MacDonald adds, "It's not uncommon to have students sign up for one course to acquire a new skill. They then might go on to receive an associate

degree and transfer to a college or university. Frequently, they come to us believing that college isn't for them, but they end up with a two-year associate degree. Other students use Kilian as a springboard to a bachelor's degree."

Kilian's varied degree offerings include accounting, management, marketing, legal assistant, fire science, and human services. Specialized programs in secretarial training and general education are also available. Kilian's academic year includes five terms composed of day and evening classes. Flexibility in scheduling allows students to enroll in the specific courses they need.

REACHING OUT TO THE LOCAL BUSINESS COMMUNITY

Kilian reaches out to the local business community for assistance in originating new courses. "We continuously monitor businesses to determine the course work and training Kilian can provide for the future," MacDonald says. "We're already doing distinct programs with US West and the fire department, and we are meeting with other businesses to examine their individual requirements."

MacDonald attributes Kilian's 95 percent placement rate to the college's emphasis on training for jobs that already exist and the quality of the education those students receive. "We try to make sure each graduate has experience working in his or her career path during the educational process," he says. "We want them to feel they can leave here and go right to work with no surprises about their career choice."

The highest praise for Kilian, and the greatest source for new student referrals, comes from graduates of the college. "Kilian Community College has opened many doors for me in all aspects of my life," says Heather Torberson, a 1991 executive secretary graduate who is now personnel coordinator at Uniforce Temporary Services. "The staff and instructors cared about all areas of my life. I owe my greatest thanks to Kilian for where I am today."

I T STARTED WITH AN IDEA TO MAKE USE OF LAND while preserving it, and to allow people to live on the land without destroying it. Begun in 1984, the Prairie Tree development in Sioux Falls has been an unquestionable success. ♦ The project was the inspiration of Phil Helland, a biologist, horticulturist, and president of Landscape Garden Centers. In the early 1980s, he put together a proposal for

developing 218 acres of rolling hills and native prairie land on the southern edge of the city, land which belonged to the family of the late Ralph "Dude" Rogers.

Helland hoped to create a housing development that would preserve the beauty of the land, in part by planting 10,000 trees. Half of them would be harvested for Helland's landscape business, and the remainder would be left

The project got under way with Helland, Rogers, and her daughter, Jan Rogers Morlino, as the original members of Prairie Tree Partners. Five additional partners were selected for the expertise they brought to the venture: Pat and Emmet Rogers, realtors; Dick Sayre, engineer; John Van De Walle, architect; and Craig Lloyd, developer.

Prairie Tree Partners stresses in the development's building covenants that architectural designs should be simple and plain, so that homes will blend rather than contrast with the landscape. "We stress the use of natural materials," says Helland, "and insist on wood shingle or shake roofs. With the rolling hills, many of the houses look down on the rooftops of other homes. We wanted the colors of all the houses to blend with the natural colors of the prairie."

He adds, "Preserving the contours of the land presents some challenges, because the homes are often built on a slope. Because of the rolling terrain, we have to watch out for erosion during the construction phase."

Prairie Tree amenities include not only a view of the prairie to the south and the many trees planted on the hillsides and throughout the development, but also a seven-acre private park with playground equipment and picnic tables. A mile-long nature trail also winds through the homesites.

The success of Prairie Tree, which has been heralded as one of the outstanding environmental development projects in the area, has prompted the partners to consider a sequel. The Prairie Green development is currently in the planning stages as a residential community with homes along the fairways of a challenging 18-hole golf course, as well as some office facilities. "The concept is new to this part of the country," Helland says, "but it has been very successful in other regions."

Current plans call for ground to be broken in the fall of 1992 for Prairie Green, which will lie directly east of Prairie Tree. The environmental harmony that marks the original development will be repeated in its sister community of homes.

According to Helland, the success of Prairie Tree has been a combination of the beauty of the land itself, acceptance of the planned-use concept, and hours and hours of hard work put in by all of the partners. Thanks to the partnership that created Prairie Tree, families are experiencing the fulfillment of a dream.

◀ CHUCK GUSTAFSON

Homes in the Prairie Tree development are designed to blend rather than contrast with the landscape.

LIVING IN HARMONY WITH NATURE

The land was divided into 200 low-density lots. Today, eight years into the project, 120 lots have been sold, and the development is three years ahead of projections made in 1984. "Prairie Tree represents one of the last areas of good land close to the city," says Helland. "But we didn't know people would take to our idea of living in harmony with nature so fast and with such enthusiasm."

to enhance the development. In 1984, he presented his proposal to Libby Rogers, owner of the land and widow of Ralph Rogers, and she approved.

"Libby Rogers has a strong sense of the history of the land," Helland says. "Her home, adjacent to Prairie Tree, is the site of a renovated dairy barn, which preserves the heritage of the original farm."

DAKOTACARE, THE HEALTH CARE PLAN OF THE SOUTH Dakota Medical Association, is helping people throughout the state put a cap on medical costs, not medical care. As a health maintenance organization (HMO), DAKOTACARE monitors the delivery of health care services to help lower costs and control monthly premiums for its enrollees. While DAKOTACARE is the only organization of its

kind in South Dakota, over 60 percent of the nation's major employers currently offer managed care through HMOs.

According to Kirk Zimmer, senior vice president of DAKOTACARE, HMOs are fast becoming the best health care option for the '90s. "We have over 22,000 enrollees statewide," he says, "and we're growing all the time. With more than 40 different products in five categories, we offer a health care plan at a cost that fits just about any employer's needs."

QUALITY AND AFFORDABILITY

Through a variety of unique programs, DAKOTACARE strives to offer the most affordable group health coverage possible without sacrificing quality care. For example, the firm places a strong emphasis on wellness education for both enrollees and their physicians. DAKOTACARE provides special kits full of useful information on developing and maintaining a healthy lifestyle. Additional books are available on child care, aging, and personal health maintenance. A monthly newsletter also presents topics of interest in all phases of wellness. "We can help people save money by teaching them how to be wise consumers of health care," Zimmer says. "Nationally, $3 in medical care costs are saved for every $1 that is invested in this wellness education program."

Another of DAKOTACARE's goals is to minimize "red tape" for its customers. Once an enrollee presents his or her DAKOTACARE card at a clinic, hospital, or pharmacy, all claim forms are handled directly by the provider and DAKOTACARE. This "no paperwork program" saves time for the patient and the employer and enhances the speed and accuracy of claims handling.

As a managed care company, DAKOTACARE enlists a variety of other strategies to contain costs, including pre-admission notification. To help avoid unnecessary hospitalization, DAKOTACARE asks a series of questions prior to admission, such as "Is the surgical procedure really necessary?" and "Should services be performed in the hospital or at an outpatient facility?"

During an enrollee's hospital stay, DAKOTACARE, in cooperation with the doctor and hospital, continuously monitors patient care to recommend an appropriate length of stay. The company's discharge planning and individual case management services consider all factors in determining the proper time to discharge the patient and the necessary care following hospitalization. In addition, DAKOTACARE monitors prescriptions to assure that the appropriate medication is given and to determine if a generic substitute can be used to save the patient money.

MEETING CHANGING NEEDS IN SOUTH DAKOTA

DAKOTACARE's 45 employees work together to coordinate an array of services designed to keep health care costs down for thousands of South Dakota residents today and in the future. According to Zimmer, a unique combination of computer equipment and dedicated medical professionals make it all possible. "We have a full-time medical director and two part-time physician consultants on staff," he says. "They consult with other physicians on cases, conduct reviews, and keep the program abreast of new technology, drugs, and procedures. In addition, three full-time registered nurses communicate with hospitals,

monitoring cases through our concurrent review program and auditing hospital claims."

Building on seven years of experience in the health care industry, DAKOTACARE is currently exploring a variety of innovative ways to expand its offerings to accommodate the changing needs of South Dakotans. "Right now, we can write policies for groups as small as five people," Zimmer says. "We have not yet become involved in any individual policies, but that's a potential area for growth in the future."

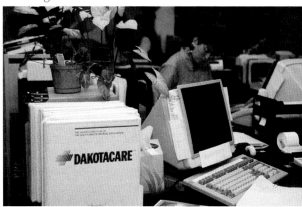

DAKOTACARE's employees monitor health care for thousands of South Dakota residents.

DAKOTACARE is also developing workers' compensation plans, programs for self-insured companies, and flexible benefit plans. In 1991, the company introduced DAKOTACARE Select, which provides a variety of deductible options for employers who want to tailor their benefits packages to fit their unique needs and desired levels of cost sharing. Under all DAKOTACARE programs, enrollees can also benefit from various amounts of group term life and disability insurance.

Clearly, innovation is an important part of DAKOTACARE's commitment to quality health care at the lowest possible cost. "We're always looking for the best way to bring consistently excellent care to our enrollees at affordable costs," says Zimmer. "The quality of our products and our focus on providing outstanding service are the main reasons we are continuing to grow today."

THE ENORMOUS DATA MEMORY OF TODAY'S MICRO-computers, the familiar PCs that sit on desks in homes and businesses around the world, is contained on a spinning disc that revolves over 150 times faster than an LP record. As the disc spins, a technological marvel called a "read-write head" flies over its surface, supported by a thin tongue of metal, at just six to eight microinches from the

surface of the disc. With the high speeds and precise distances involved, there's not much room for error—and everything depends on that tiny metal strip.

Hutchinson Technology, Inc., with a Sioux Falls presence since 1988, manufactures nearly 70 percent of those indispensable metal strips used worldwide in the suspension systems of the common disc drive.

Founded in Hutchinson, Minnesota in 1965, the company began producing microcomputer disc suspension assemblies in the early 1980s. With over 800 employees at its production facility in Sioux Falls, Hutchinson Technology has been one of the area's fastest growing firms and one of the most impressive high-tech enterprises ever established in the community.

A STRONG PEOPLE ORIENTATION

The company's rapid growth is not surprising, given the boom in the production and use of microcomputers throughout the 1980s. But the secret to Hutchinson's success—the company has garnered almost 70 percent of the global market share—lies with its employees, says Lee Olson, vice president of Sioux Falls operations.

"We have a strong people orientation," he explains. "It's easy to think that high-tech enterprises are very technologically oriented, but we rely on human interaction and human solutions. We utilize a very participative management system with an open door policy at all levels of the company—and it pays off."

> "We have a strong people orientation," explains Lee Olson, vice president of Sioux Falls operations. "It's easy to think that high-tech enterprises are very technologically oriented, but we rely on human interaction and human solutions."

In fact, many of the most exciting advances in HTI company policy and production processes come not from computer engineers working on abstruse equations late into the night, but from "focus teams" within the company. Composed of a cross section of all working levels, these groups bring their imagination and experience to bear on new challenges and old problems alike. Over 28 focus teams, whose members range from custodians to engineers, have successfully tackled complex issues and emerged with innovative solutions.

Another key element in employee involvement is the IDEAS program—Improvement Driven By Employees Assures Success. In addition to those

generated by the ongoing work of the focus teams, about 175 original ideas are submitted to the program each month. The company also offers tuition reimbursement as a benefit to encourage employees to sharpen their skills through education and increase individual contributions to the company's success.

Clearly, Hutchinson Technology takes very seriously its corporate vision statement: "Our people are the source of our strength, and we will treat them with the highest regard."

QUALITY CONTROL, CUSTOMER SATISFACTION

Attention to detail and a sense of teamwork are crucial in an industry that works in microscopic increments and measures its quality control in parts per million. An error of one-sixth of a degree in a suspension assembly head can cause a costly computer crash. To minimize error and upgrade quality, Hutchinson Technology has already installed $18 million in automated manufacturing equipment and $2 million in building improvements since opening the Sioux Falls plant in 1988. All of these advances are aimed at ensuring that the suspension assemblies made by this global leader are the world's best.

"Our engineers work directly with the design engineers of the computer companies who use our products,"

Olson says. "We now make 15 different types of suspensions with up to 200 variations. Each is a distinctive and unique part that is critical to the success of the disk drive. Between our Sioux Falls and Minnesota plants, we make 140 million suspension assemblies annually. With that kind of volume, minimizing error is a major concern of everyone at Hutchinson."

An integral part of the HTI corporate vision is striving for consistent customer satisfaction; at Hutchinson Technology, it's an obsession. And as the computer industry keeps changing, HTI must also change, staying abreast of customer needs and product innovations to maintain its market leadership. For example, HTI has responded

quickly to the trend toward a global marketplace. Today, 70 percent of the company's production output is shipped to Pacific Rim and European countries.

"We walk two paths," Olson says. "Although the personal computer industry has slowed down, the disc drive industry is still growing as new software is developed. Much of this new software is very memory-intensive, gobbling up space on disc drives and necessitating large capacity drives, which require new or different suspension assemblies. We need to stay in touch with new technology in every area of our business."

But in the midst of its high-tech surroundings, as Hutchinson engineers help push the limits of tomorrow's computers even further, the Sioux Falls residents who work at HTI and make the future possible have a simpler view of things.

"Although over 800 people are employed here," says Steve Kary, an HTI employee, "there really is the feeling of a 'mom and pop' type of business. No one is too special to talk to. That's a very rare trait for a business of this size."

Through human interaction and human solutions, HTI has made great strides in an often impersonal high-tech industry. That people orientation, which inspires hundreds of Hutchinson employees every day, promises to keep the company focused on a bright future in Sioux Falls and across the globe.

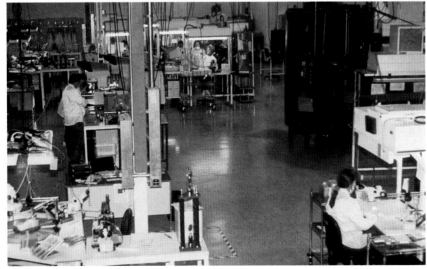

Above and opposite: Since 1988, Hutchinson Technology has been an important high-tech enterprise in Sioux Falls where it employs over 800 local residents.

Top: As part of HTI's emphasis on team-based problem solving, this group was charged with developing and implementing solutions to airborne contamination within the manufacturing area.

THIRTY YEARS AGO IT WAS ONLY A PATIENT'S DREAM: to undergo surgery and return home in a single day. Today, same-day surgery is the sole specialty of the Sioux Falls Surgical Center, a 30,000-square-foot facility established in 1985. ♦ "The Sioux Falls Surgical Center, unlike many other health care facilities, is not faced with trying to divert its efforts in several different directions," says

Dr. Don Schellpfeffer, medical director and one of the founders of the center. "The unique focus of our facility allows us to direct all of our human and economic resources toward one goal—quality ambulatory surgery."

Thanks to same-day surgery—also known as ambulatory or outpatient surgery—patients can undergo a surgi-

cal procedure, spend an appropriate amount of time in a recovery area, and be discharged by the end of the day to recuperate at home or, in some cases, return to their daily routine.

"Ambulatory surgery is a relatively new concept which began in Phoenix in 1970," Schellpfeffer says. "The growth of the industry has been helped by Medicare and other third-party payers, such as insurance companies, who have directed same-day surgery for certain procedures to decrease the cost to patients."

While the Sioux Falls Surgical Center prides itself on being a value-oriented medical facility, Nursing Director Mary Sturm says the patient's well-being is the primary consideration in every case. "The welfare of our patients is never compromised through their choice of a same-day procedure," she says. "The safety and comfort of the patient is our main concern."

A RANGE OF SAME-DAY SURGICAL OPTIONS

The range of same-day surgical options available at the Sioux Falls Surgical Center covers the medical spectrum. From plastic surgery to tonsillectomy, from urology to orthopedic surgery, and from eye surgery to dental work, physicians schedule virtually every type of procedure, including laser surgery.

One procedure not offered anywhere else in the Sioux Falls area is Extracorporeal Shockwave Lithotripsy (ESWL), a unique, high-tech treatment for the removal of kidney stones. This safe, reliable procedure uses computer-aimed shockwaves generated outside the body to pulverize kidney stones so they can pass harmlessly from the body.

"Medical equipment and technology are very dynamic," says Schellpfeffer. "They are constantly changing. But we try to anticipate the needs of our patients and the physicians who use our facility, and to keep up-to-date in both equipment and technology."

COMMITTED TO PATIENT SATISFACTION

A dedicated staff of 70 combined with top quality equipment housed in a newly expanded facility has proven to be a successful mix at the Sioux Falls Surgical Center, where as many as 40 procedures are performed every day. In fact, the center ranks in the top 5 percent among independent ambulatory surgery centers in the United States based on number of procedures performed annually.

According to Sturm, satisfied patients in the Sioux Falls area have come back to the center for as many as 10 different procedures. She cites the staff's strong commitment to personal attention as an important part of the center's appeal. Dr. Schellpfeffer, an anesthesiologist, not only works with every case but also phones each patient after surgery to answer questions and reassure the patient. "That call from the doctor the next day helps tremendously," says Sturm. "It's a question of contact. Patients need to feel that the physician cares about their well-being."

Even the physical layout of the center is designed with the patient in mind. A U-shaped building, the facility brings patients in one door to a comfortable waiting area, but discharges them through a separate exit adjacent to the recovery rooms. This separation of pre- and post-operative patients significantly reduces the anxiety level for everyone. "The anxiety associated with surgery is high enough," Schellpfeffer says. "We assure the privacy of our post-operative patients and help keep our pre-op patients calm."

That kind of attention to detail, along with a professional staff and state-of-the-art facility, has made the Sioux Falls Surgical Center an indispensable part of the regional medical community.

A dedicated staff of 70 combined with top quality equipment housed in a newly expanded facility has proven to be a successful mix at the Sioux Falls Surgical Center.

SINCE ITS FOUNDING IN 1988, CELLULAR ONE OF Sioux Falls has been in the business of person-to-person communication. Today, people no longer have to call places, they can call other people, explains Laurie Arthur, company controller. And that's the bottom line in modern cellular service. ♦ "If you're in Minneapolis, and someone in Sioux Falls dials your number," says Arthur, "your

Perhaps the greatest benefit of cellular phone service is the increased productivity cellular clients experience.

phone will ring in Minneapolis, not at home in Sioux Falls. Cellular technology is smart enough to find you just about anywhere. In the event you don't want to be found, you can simply turn the phone off, then turn it on again when you need to be in touch. Messages can be left by the calling party when the phone is in the 'off' mode and later retrieved by the cellular telephone subscriber. Cellular One offers this convenient voice mail feature to all subscribers."

GROWTH IN TECHNOLOGY

In recent years, growth in technology has been a key to the proliferation of cellular communications nationwide. When the service first came to Sioux Falls, cellular phone equipment was much more expensive, and the technology was fairly new. Today, the equipment is so affordable that many families install cellular telephones in their vehicles just for emergency use.

"The technology today is working on reducing the size of the unit and making the batteries last longer," says Arthur. "Dick Tracy wrist watch units may still be in the future, but we're getting much closer."

For example, the new Motorola Digital Personal Communicator, a personal telephone sold locally by Cellular One, fits easily into a pocket or purse. Although it weighs just 12.3 ounces, the unit doesn't scrimp on features. This technological marvel includes a seven-digit color LED display, tone dialing from a keypad or the 101-number memory, auto redial, super speed dialing, and more.

With such small units, customers can take their phones virtually everywhere—and cellular service has managed to keep pace. "Our area of service is Minnehaha County only," Arthur says, "but our cellular equipment will

process calls anywhere there's service. These days, that's just about everywhere in the United States."

Low-power radio transmitter towers, called cell sites, ensure clear, comprehensive cellular service to Minnehaha County. Outside Sioux Falls, Cellular One is affiliated with a Regional Roaming Network, which provides reduced roaming rates in the five-state region.

Cellular One of Sioux Falls began service in February 1988, after being licensed by the Federal Communications Commission as one of only two cellular services in Minnehaha County. Today, the company has 14 employees, including sales, administrative, technical, and clerical staff. From its headquarters in the Airport Industrial Park, the young firm sells mostly Uniden and

> "A cellular telephone is not an expensive toy, but a vital tool in a wide range of businesses," says Laurie Arthur, controller.

Motorola cellular equipment, but can order virtually anything to meet the special needs of its customers.

Three basic types of cellular telephones are currently on the market: transportable cellular phones, which boast the power and range of a mobile unit but can be moved from one vehicle to another; mobile units, which are designed to be mounted in a vehicle; and handheld cellular phones, which are small enough to be carried everywhere with their owners. According to Arthur, about half of Cellular One's customers use mobile cellular phones in their vehicles, while the remainder—such as contractors, builders, and professionals who spend time away from the office but out of the vehicle—use portable units.

A VITAL BUSINESS TOOL

Perhaps the greatest benefit of cellular phone service is not the convenience of having a telephone within reach at all times, but the increased productivity cellular clients experience. "Because cellular technology causes such a profound increase in productivity," Arthur says, "our customers find the cost of the equipment and service to be nearly insignificant. A cellular telephone is not an expensive toy, but a vital tool in a wide range of businesses."

This convenient technology is no longer applied only to telephone communication. Cellular customers can now utilize a facsimile machine in their vehicles, or hook up a cellular phone to a modem to transmit computer data. "Cellular telephones allow people to communicate almost anywhere, anytime," says Arthur. "The day will come when every person has a telephone at all times. Cellular technology won't replace land line service, but will supplement it for even better interpersonal communication."

And as communication emerges as a watchword for the 21st century, Cellular One of Sioux Falls is proud to be a part of this exciting national trend.

SINCE ITS FOUNDING IN 1989, CHARTER HOSPITAL OF Sioux Falls has pursued a primary mission: to be the leading regional provider of quality behavioral health services. But Charter Administrator John Olson points out another, equally important goal. ♦ "We are trying to destigmatize mental health problems," he says. "We're proud of what we are doing in the area of community education. Through

our free seminars and support of community activities, we let people know there are ways to find help for their problems."

Charter's theme, "If you don't get help at Charter, please get help somewhere," illustrates the hospital's dedication to addressing the needs of area residents. "We have filled a need in the community and in the region for specialized behavioral health services," says Olson. "And in doing so, we have shown people that help is available in a confidential, hopeful, and professional setting."

A CONTINUUM OF CARE

Charter Hospital of Sioux Falls is a 60-bed facility with active outpatient and resident programs for children, teens, and adults. The hospital's 150-employee staff includes six attending psychiatrists and 20 consulting physicians. A fully equipped gym, relaxing lounge areas, contemporary living quarters, and group activity rooms highlight Charter's attractive, modern facility on South Louise Avenue.

For each resident patient, the hospital's comprehensive "continuum of care" begins with a needs assessment that includes personal interaction with a health care professional. Each patient is assigned a primary caregiver, who heads an interdisciplinary treatment team which daily assesses the patient's needs, develops short- and long-term treatment goals, and helps bring about stabilization—the beginning of recovery. The patient is then ready to participate in the many other services available at the hospital, ranging from the Partial Hospitalization program, which brings the patient into the facility for a predetermined length of time each weekday, to outpatient counseling services at the Charter Counseling Center.

In all Charter programs, the family plays an important role in virtually every phase of the treatment process. Children participate in "family day," workshops, and individual therapy, while educational groups and lifeskills classes teach valuable social skills and help them keep up with school work.

A fully equipped gym, relaxing lounge areas, contemporary living quarters, and group activity rooms highlight Charter's attractive, modern facility on South Louise Avenue.

Through the Family Focus program, Charter's adolescents and their families undergo an orientation session and complete weekly assignments designed to bring the family into the treatment process. Parent support groups and family therapy sessions also complement the recovery program. Follow-up outpatient care includes weekly group therapy sessions and coordination with a variety of key individuals outside the family, such as teachers, physicians, and clergy members.

Adult programs include special topics groups, individual therapy sessions, and regular professional treatment team meetings to help the patient set goals and reflect on progress.

OUTPATIENT AND COMMUNITY EDUCATIONAL SERVICES

Outpatient and community educational services are available through Charter Counseling Services located on East 26th Street. Specialized therapy groups assist patients in dealing with stress, anxiety, anger, and recovery from sexual abuse. Likewise, growth groups for adolescents from ages 13 to 18 and support group meetings for victims of panic disorder and attention deficit disorder are held at the center.

Charter Hospital reaches out to thousands of area residents through free community workshops scheduled regularly at the center. A variety of interesting topics have been addressed, including post-holiday depression, birth order and personality styles, the aftermath of suicide, and the underachieving child. The hospital also operates Charter Institute, which offers continuing education opportunities to health care and other professionals in behavioral and mental health areas.

In an effort to extend its service area, Charter provides traveling workshops in nearby communities like Mitchell, Watertown, and Rapid City. Likewise, clinical staff are available to speak on mental health issues through the Charter Speakers Bureau and through in-service programs.

"By doing all we can in the area of education, we are fulfilling our mission," says Olson. "Even if just one person hears the message—that help is available—and takes that first step to change his or her life, then we've done our job."

▲ RON BOWDEN

T HE LAND DREW THOUSANDS OF IMMIGRANT FARMERS to the Dakota prairie in the late 1800s. As their families arrived, the new settlers established churches and schools, the cornerstones of community. Soon, it was evident that higher education would also be a necessity. ◆ In that forward-looking spirit, Huron University was born in 1883. The university was incorporated in Huron, South Dakota

in April of that year. In May 1887, the institution granted the first college degree in the Dakota Territory. Today, the private university still operates its main campus in Huron, as well as branch campuses in Sioux Falls, London, England, and Tokyo, Japan.

FROM HURON TO LONDON

The main campus, with 500 graduate and undergraduate students, serves the heartland of southeastern South Dakota, offering associate and bachelor's degrees through a variety of programs: business administration, elementary and secondary education, and education with a focus on history, biology, social science, business, and physical education/coaching. Other programs in-

Huron's Sioux Falls campus serves nearly 200 non-traditional adult students in a variety of degree courses.

clude nursing, human services, criminal justice, applied management, communications/public relations, computer/business, general studies, and travel and tourism. The university's Huron campus also offers the Master of Business Administration degree.

In addition to being the first institution of higher learning to grant a degree in the Dakotas, Huron University has the longest continuous record of accreditation by the North Central Association

of Colleges and Schools (NCA) among private colleges in the Dakotas. The university is also approved for training elementary and secondary school teachers by the state Division of Education, and its associate degree of nursing program is accredited by the National League for Nursing and approved by the South Dakota Board of Nursing.

In the spring of 1990, Huron University opened a branch campus in London, England. The London campus, which today has an enrollment in excess of 300 students, offers bachelor's degrees in business administration with a concentration in the areas of international management, marketing, and economics/finance; European studies; humanities; applied management; and

art history. London students of the university may also earn the Master of Business Administration degree.

The Tokyo, Japan branch campus was approved by NCA in August 1992. More than 300 students were enrolled for the fall semester.

EXPANDING TO SIOUX FALLS

Recognizing the rapid growth of Sioux Falls—the largest city in South Dakota—and its role as a regional medical, retail, and financial center, the university opened a local branch campus in January 1991 at 2900 East 26th Street. Already an important part of the Sioux

In January 1991, Huron University established a branch campus in Sioux Falls.

Falls community, the campus serves more than 200 non-traditional adult students in degree courses ranging from business administration, applied management, and accounting to humanities, social sciences, and computer literacy.

In response to a continual growth in student enrollment, the Sioux Falls campus expanded during its first year. According to the director of the university's Sioux Falls campus, the institution expects the current enrollment numbers to remain stable.

"We anticipate maintaining an enrollment of 200-plus adult students taking classes in three major areas of study: accounting, business administration, and applied management," the director says. "We're also considering the possibility of offering an MBA here at some future date. Two of our other campuses already offer that degree option."

From the dream of American pioneers to the alma mater of tomorrow's business leaders, Huron University has strived to be an educational leader in South Dakota for over a century. Through its expansions to London, Tokyo, and Sioux Falls, the university has made a further commitment to the needs of today's students.

PHOTO EDITORS
JOEL AND LAVONNE STRASSER

Joel E. Strasser has been an architectural and advertising photographer since 1958 with assignments throughout the United States. He attended Augustana College in Sioux Falls, the Progressive School of Photography in New Haven, Connecticut, and served with the United States Air Force.

Strasser is a Master of Photography and Photographic Craftsmen by the Professional Photographers of America, a member of American Society of Photographers, South Dakota Professional Photographers, and Cameracraftsmen of America. He has served as a national judge, spoken at national conventions in the United States and Canada, and taught at many photography schools.

Strasser's sensitive photography, done for the love of it, has sold to many collectors of fine photography. Since 1988, his wife, Lavonne, has also become involved in the publishing of much of Joel's photography. His most well known titles are *Where My Heart Is*, *South Dakota 100*, and *The Newton Hills*.

PAUL BUCKOWSKI, originally of Saranac Lake, New York, graduated from the Rochester Institute of Technology in 1989. He joined the staff of the *Argus Leader* in May 1990.

BILL CARLSON has owned Carlson Photography for 15 years. His images are distributed through Think Visuals, a stock image studio, and he specializes in outdoor action, industrial, and underwater photography, and film. Carlson has won both the Gold Camera and the Silver Screen Awards from the U.S. Industrial Film Festival and also awards from the Chicago and Houston Film Festivals.

BRUCE CHRISTIANSON owns Christianson Studios, PhotoLogic, which is oriented to electronic desktop publishing, direct digital image capture, enhancement, and creative image manipulation. Christianson, who is represented by Think Visuals, is a Minnesota advertising photographer of 20 years. He has produced award-winning photos for annual reports, brochures, calendars, and magazine ads, as well as multimedia for nationwide agencies and clients.

LLOYD CUNNINGHAM has been a news photographer with the *Argus Leader* for 22 years. A consistent winner of news, feature, and portrait awards, he majored in photojournalism at the University of Iowa. Cunningham and his wife have raised a son and daughter in Sioux Falls.

BILL GOEHRING has worked as a photographer and videographer for Media One Advertising/Marketing since 1989. He has received several Addy Awards and placed second in the United Way's Annual Photography Competition for 1991-1992. Goehring is currently pursuing social issue projects on several South Dakota Indian reservations.

ROBERT J. GRIPP, a native of Sioux Falls, has been a free-lance photographer since 1981, and opened his own studio, High Exposure, in 1987. His work ranges from commercial, architectural, and promotional to scenic, art, and dance photography. As a professional musician of 25 years, Gripp has also developed many band promotional projects.

BILL HAINES, originally of San Francisco, received his B.S. in News-Editorial Journalism from the University of Oregon. He joined the *Argus Leader* in January of 1991, where he pursues editorial photography. Haines' photos have been published in *Newsweek*, *Fortune*, *Money*, the *New York Times*, and the *Dallas Morning News*.

DAN JENSEN, a graduate of Colorado Mountain College Commercial Photography School in 1981, has been a free-lance commercial photographer for the last 11 years. A Sioux Falls native, Jensen participated in a two-man exhibition, Urban Images, with Antonio M. Sanchez in 1990.

ROD JONES, a life-long resident of Sioux Falls, opened his studio, Custom Color, 13 years ago. Before turning to photography, Jones worked in medical management. His commercial work includes studio and on-site corporate advertising, architectural, and public relations photography,

MARIANNE LARSEN was born in Los Angeles and received her B.A. in 1963 from Scripps College in Claremont, California. She moved to Sioux Falls in 1966, and opened her own studio, As I See It, in 1987. Larsen's work has been exhibited at the Civic Fine Arts Center and at Gallery 306 in Sioux Falls, and she has twice won competitions sponsored by *Minnesota Monthly* magazine.

MILO and ELLIE OLSEN opened Olsen Photography, a studio specializing in portraiture, in 1983. Milo Olsen grew up in Sioux Falls and received an Associates Degree in Applied Science from the University of South Dakota in Springfield. Ellie attended Wayne State University in Nebraska. The Olsens live in Sioux Falls with their one child.

MIKE ROEMER, originally of Green Bay, Wisconsin, graduated from the University of Wisconsin in communications and photography in 1986. He joined the staff of the *Argus Leader* in 1988, doing general assignment photojournalism. Roemer won the Best of Gannett in 1991, first place in color photography for a newspaper with over 40,000 circulation.

ANTONIO M. SANCHEZ, originally from Mexico, came to Sioux Falls in 1985 to work as a photographer for an advertising agency. He opened his own studio, Sanchez Photography, with his wife, Julie, in 1990. The Sanchezes specialize in advertising, corporate, and industrial photography.

KIRBY SCHULTZ, with twenty years experience in creation, design, and photography, is now a partner of Henkin Schultz advertising agency. Schultz has worked on commercial assignments in Japan and the Phillipines, and at the Indianapolis 500, the Winter Olymics, and Mount Rushmore. He has received several advertising awards, including the Lifetime Achievement Award from the South Dakota Advertising Federation.

DAVE SONNICHSEN, a native of Sioux Falls, has been a free-lance photographer since his active duty in the military began in 1969. A teacher at the South Dakota School for the Deaf since 1976, Sonnichsen assists the staff as a media specialist in all areas of audio/visual support. Sonnichsen is also the N.C.O.I.C. (Non- Commissioned Officer in Charge) of the South Dakota Air National Guard Visual Information Section.

KEN STARKENBURG, an amateur photographer, performs wedding and portrait photography on a part-time basis. He has been a member of the Sioux Falls Camera Club for 22 years and is its current president. Starkenburg has won many awards in the club's monthly competitions and in an eleven state area.

TIM STEINBERG, originally of Sioux Falls, has lived in St. Paul, Minnesota since 1981, where he has worked on a free-lance basis with Stonemountain Photography for eight years. His photography is marketed by Think Visuals, a stock image agency, and he specializes in travel photography, shooting hotel properties for travel brochures in the airline industry. Steinberg's 1992 credits include *National Geographic*, NFL Superbowl programs, BBC Television, and the television series, "Northern Exposure."

On a hot August afternoon, what child can resist the urge to dangle her feet in the cool water that trickles over the rocks near the falls?

SPIRIT OF
SIOUX FALLS
INDEX OF PATRONS

Anyone who grew up on the South Dakota prairie pays attention to weather. When thunderheads climb the western sky to block the sun on a summer afternoon, folks know rain is coming. A red sunset often means a quiet night and clear morning.